TetraMap®

How to Develop People & Business
the Way Nature Intended

By
Yoshimi & Jon Brett

Orders	www.tetramap.com E-mail: info@tetramap.com
Published By	TETRAMAP INTERNATIONAL LIMITED 5 Island View Terrace Howick Auckland New Zealand Tel 64- 9- 535 6582 Fax 64- 9- 535 6578 www.tetramap.com
Authors	Yoshimi Brett yoshimi@tetramap.com Jon Brett jon@tetramap.com
ISBN	0-9582143-2-8
Edition	Edition 1.0, May 2002 Re-printed February 2003 Re-printed August 2004 with minor corrections.
Printing	Printed in New Zealand Pages printed on 100% recycled paper produced entirely from post consumer waste, without the use of any chlorine bleaching processes. Cover on 75% recycled paper.

Contents

Contents

Contents

Acknowledgments

The TetraMap® is part of a long journey. After 20 years, we are only at the beginning.

Thanks and gratitude to our:

Guides:
Buckminster Fuller, Old Chinese, Glynn Braddy, John Hulbert, Robert Kiyosaki, Dr. Amy Edmondson.

Supportive clients and colleagues:
Michele Hartson, Angela Griffin, Jamie Delich, Dave Lee, Mel Martin, Harry and Di Baruhas, John Williams, Linda Bowen, Rosa Martha Girón, Héctor Efraín Rodríguez, Jacqui Hofmann, Val Jackson, Leslie Hamilton, Noel Atkinson the Printer, Dave Gunson the Artist, and all the wonderful TetraMap Facilitators around the world.

Champion teams:
Bill Wilson and the QEI team, John Davies and the TrainingPoint.Net team, Bobbi DePorter and the Learning Forum team, Graham Harvey and Team 7.

Reviewers:
Special thanks to two people we have yet to meet in person, but who committed time and energy to giving us all-important feedback. Ned Hamson, Tony Pattinson.

Foreword

By Michele Hartson, May 2002

Most of my adult life, I have worked with nonprofit organizations assisting low-income communities with issues concerning housing, childcare, community safety, and jobs. In this type of work, people working in community development talk about the diversity in a neighborhood; race, class, gender and age are usually the things considered. We have built programs to help communities "work" on all of these issues.

What I have come to appreciate in my time working with the TetraMap of Nature, is that race, class gender and age are only some of the factors that contribute to our true diversity. There is much more to diversity. Diversity, in fact, is a big part of everyone's daily life, yet most of us are either oblivious to it, or we choose to ignore it. Diversity is a result of our behavior. We are more who we are largely because of how we behave. This program gives us a new way to understand and appreciate that fact.

Yoshimi and Jon Brett, through their work in developing this model, have given us a new way to examine and find our own answers for the question - *Why are you like that?* Through this new lens we can see that there is a lot more to diversity than the factors of age, sex, race and class. We, like the tetrahedron which serves as the metaphor for the model, are very complex systems; we have a lot going on in our lives, and we demonstrate that complexity in our personal interactions.

The information in this book will give you a new way to look at human behavior and social interaction. It will give you a new appreciation for the real diversity that we have in our homes, schools, places of worship and workplaces. The new way to look at behavior is through the natural elements of earth, air, water, and fire. As humans, we all have behaviors that coincide with the four Elements, and we all have the ability to demonstrate these behaviors when the need arises, but we indeed have our own individual and preferred way of being. With the TetraMap, you will come to understand how the various combinations of behaviors make us who we are. This system illuminates the areas in which we are strong and at the same time, provides for us the areas where we can grow to better work with others.

I have found in using and conducting training sessions with hundreds of people using this model, that it is very intuitive. This program is powerful in helping people with the realization of themselves, and to see others in a new light. I have seen people experience very profound insights regarding their own behavior, and the behavior of others in just a matter of hours. I have witnessed strained relationships being put at ease, and watched with awe as people made new commitments to work at understanding each other better.

When people come to the point of being able to understand each other's strengths and see how those strengths in turn can be engaged to build a relationship instead of letting the differences between people act as separators, then powerful things happen. Teams become more productive, personal relationships become closer. Simply speaking, people just get along better. These are impressive and profound outcomes for the investment of just a few hours. I have found it to be life changing for me in terms of how I now look at the behavior of others and how I adjust my behavior to improve communication and build mutual respect.

I hope you find this information as useful and powerful as I have. My wholehearted and deepest wish, is that in searching for the answer to the question *Why are you like that?* you will be able to use the information you obtain along the way to grow, and improve all the relationships in your life.

Michele Hartson

Michele is the Director of Learn@ Enterprise at The Enterprise Foundation in Columbia, Maryland.

Overview

> *Love your limitations, but choose them wisely.*
> Yodimi

This book is about choosing how to relate to others.

Remember Yoda from the movie Star Wars? Yodimi is Yoda's Grandmother. Contrary to popular opinion that *there are no limitations*, Yodimi suggests that we will always have limitations...the challenge is choosing the ones you want! We always make choices when we relate to others. We can choose to *react* as we have usually done in the past, or we can choose to *respond* appropriately to the current unique situation.

The TetraMap is a model that simplifies the complex. It maps the complexity of Nature into four basic Elements: Earth, Air, Water and Fire. Then, using the power of metaphor we apply the map to human behavior. The TetraMap helps us choose a balanced, holistic perspective; whether it is to improve relationships, strengthen teamwork, clarify a corporate vision, or provide a framework for organizational development.

The origins of the TetraMap and its evolution reveal the amazing potential to expand our perceptions of how we view each other... and in time, how we view the diverse motives and cultures of the world. Let's focus on the inherent beauty of Nature and the TetraMap, and view both in their simplest structural form... the tetrahedron.

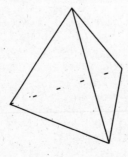

This very simple shape reflects Nature and unfolds into the TetraMap. Each side is equal and offers a different perspective, a different point from which to view the world. Yet no two perspectives oppose each other! That's the very special Nature of the TetraMap. It guides us to see ourselves, others and the world around us, from multiple perspectives. There is more to life than good/bad, black/white, yes/no, right/wrong and yet this is how we often choose to interpret our experience. Binary symmetry is the first thing we naturally look for, and when found, we seldom look further.

In the meantime, war breaks out over the shades of gray and the refusal to consider multiple perspectives. The TetraMap is a map that is intended to quell some of those wars, whether they are personal internal conflict, interpersonal strife or organizational turf wars. This book is meant to provide you with tools and hope… hope for better communication, fewer wars, respect for diversity and greater synergy in our work and life endeavors.

This book describes:

○ How Nature's Elements, Earth, Air, Water, and Fire provide a metaphor for seeing the world from at least four different perspectives.

○ How to celebrate diversity and capitalize on people's strengths.

○ How to create balanced strategies for developing business.

The TetraMap is about developing people and business the way Nature intended, through interdependent, synergistic systems. Just as Earth, Air, Water and Fire interdependently create synergy and growth, we hope that you'll use the TetraMap to guide you in your own personal journey of growth and creation.

Contents

TetraMap - How to Develop People & Business the Way Nature Intended

The Nature of Behavior

Chapter Overview

O   Natural Intentions

O   The TetraMap of Behavior

Natural Intentions

Nature surrounds us, nurtures us and may even force us to make decisions about our very existence. It is the perfect metaphor and reflection of who we are and what we can strive to be.

Nature is pervasive and is not contained by political boundaries, though politics now has much to do with overall sustainability of our planet. Nature has been used as a metaphor throughout the ages. Earth, Air, Water and Fire symbols and personifications are a part of most cultural legends and myths. We are all affected daily by Nature's work.

When we speak of down-to-earth individuals who are hands on, practical, it's easy to quickly understand what type of person this might be. We recognize the fiery nature in people who have no problem creating wild ideas and inspiring others with flair and energy. Our watery friends, who are so easily moved to tears, flow along calmly and keep us together. And others with their heads in clouds of thought and theories reflect the clarity of air.

Metaphor in the Corporation

Imagine a company event, organized to improve teamwork and performance. The meeting room is filled with managers and staff looking for answers to their questions about structure and responsibilities, about why things aren't working and about how to make team life better.

Before them are laid out photos of beautiful scenes from Nature - majestic mountains, clear skies with wisps of white clouds, peaceful and deep blue lakes, fiery sunrises and sunsets. People are immediately drawn to one or two pictures and are asked to share what it is about a particular photo that reflects them.

This is an easy assignment and participants relax a bit, but wonder what this has to do with performance improvement. Because of the different but non-threatening nature of this opening session, responses are quickly forthcoming and numerous.

> *This dark and ominous sky reminds me of me and my temperament. Lately I've been a bit moody, but see the break in the sky? There's hope.*

> *I picked this lake because, like me, I like to think I'm a calming influence on people.*

> *This jagged mountain looks like a real challenge to climb. That's what I like - a big challenge staring you in the face.*

> *Red sky in morning, sailor's warning. Red sky at night, sailor's delight. With this sunset, it's hopefully going to be a better day tomorrow!*

Nature gives us signals, reflections and lessons all the time. We're reminded constantly of the beauty she offers us, but often in our busy-ness, we by-pass the smell of the roses for money to pay the gardener. In this busy-ness, we miss the natural synergies and interdependencies that can teach us so much about how to succeed in business the way Nature intended.

Interdependence and Synergy

A common definition of synergy is the *whole is greater than the sum of its parts* or 1+1 = 3. To Buckminster Fuller, scientist, inventor, developer of the geodesic dome (1895-1983), synergy refers to *the behavior of whole systems*. This behavior he defines as unpredictable when the behaviors of the parts are considered separately.

In Nature, in the workplace, in music, in the hospital operating room, it is hoped, even strategized that the synergy created by a group significantly add to the value created by each individual. For the purpose of this book, synergy is defined as the catalyzing and unleashing of extraordinary results in an interdependent environment. Or simply, 1+1=4.

We've all seen synergy created. Be it on the playing field when the team gels and records are broken, or in a concert when the musicians are in the groove, totally in sync with each other. We've heard synergy when a choir sings like angels, in perfect harmony and time, or can imagine the synergy created when a surgical team saves a life.

Synergy is as natural as the interdependencies that create it. We see it everyday, maybe to the point of taking natural synergies for granted. So why is it so difficult to create synergy on an on-going basis? Why don't we acknowledge or foster the interdependencies within our families and organizations, if in fact we know that synergy is possible?

Silos

Synergy is created in an interdependent environment. One part need not necessarily know exactly what the other part or parts are capable of. In some cases knowing helps, in others, not knowing may be just what unleashes the extraordinary forces within each of us.

You may have in your career, observed or been a part of the *silo effect* often found in the workplace. Each silo or department, works away diligently at what they know best. Each department is skilled, capable and proud of the wisdom and synergy they have created time and time again. There is such a sense of pride in fact, that this unified team often wonders what the other so-called teams actually do to earn their place in the company.

A classic is the division between departments within an organization. They even call themselves 'divisions' as in the Sales Division, Marketing Division. Great managers often lead these teams. Great managers are often also great leaders who can muster the forces to create the kind of synergy that would make any leader proud. Often each division even has its own compelling vision and values that maintain the momentum and strengthen the team as it performs.

Such teams may knowingly understand and create synergy within an interdependent environment. However, take a step outside the silo and *bam!* Smack into another silo that seemingly attempts to thwart your every move. Sales looking at Marketing wondering where in the world *this* product came from. Marketing wondering in return how Sales could miss the opportunity to sell in the quantities predicted by diligent market research.

Meanwhile, the Customer Service Division wonders what happened to the plot and how both Sales and Marketing lost it. With little or no product knowledge, Service must feel their way in the dark to respond to customer inquiries.

Yes, all of these divisions do work for the same company. The same company that spent thousands of dollars to plan, brainstorm and strategize the promulgation of the corporate mission, vision and values. The same company that expounds values of open and honest communication, teamwork, innovation and even synergy.

The teams that do have it together, that have catalyzed synergy and gotten results, no doubt have a working understanding of the need for interdependency, trust and open communication. And yet surprisingly, silos often persist, entrenched in their own success.

Interdependent Teams

What does it mean to be a part of an interdependent team? How is trust built to the degree that synergy happens?

First consider a group of dependent people. Whether dependent on another silo, the leader, or some external entity, these people are totally incapacitated to take action. These dependent beings live comfortably in *Unlessland*.
I can't do this **unless**...

○   *They* do *their* job

○   *He* or *she* makes a decision and tells me what to do

○   *They* get *their* house in order.

○   *The government* pays...after all it's for the well being of the nation...

The problem is out-there and until it is fixed out-there, they are totally unable to move forward. This is co-dependency in the raw. Unfortunately, reliance on another is actually promulgated within many cultures. It is totally acceptable to blame others for ones own lack. They are applauded when joining the line of sheep, following and doing exactly what is asked with no questioning, no thought of cause and effect or of consequences. *Keep me ignorant, but take care of me.*

Now let's consider a group of independent people who are proud, confident, and headstrong. *I don't need anyone, just do as I say and we'll get along fine.* Independents have the luxury of choice, personal success and clarity of responsibility. They know, or hope, that at the end of the day, they can look back and say, *I did it my way.* Groups that now stand on their own with no assistance can boast of achievements and out-of-the-box thinking to have made it this far.

Like an adolescent getting the first taste of freedom, an individual, a team, or a tribe may find great energy and excitement in going it alone and proving to the world that more can be accomplished now that the apron strings are broken, or the shackles of oppression are released. It soon becomes a question of cost: What economic, social, environmental costs are we willing to pay for independence? In the end…it may cost the earth.

Newfound independence may be no different than silo mentality. Many teens, teams and tribes find themselves in the glory of independence only to find that their silo walls are cracking and crumbling. By then it may be late in the game to enroll others to join in. Answers might eventually be found in collaboration and partnerships but again, at what cost? Calculate the energy, money, or lives that have been wasted in the process, then assess the cost of independence.

Natural synergy is created in an *inter*dependent environment. Our efforts to create synergy at home and in the workplace take energy and a balance of:

○ Firm facts
○ Clear logic
○ Calm feelings
○ Bright possibilities

Creating synergy in an interdependent environment means having choice. Consider it a pre-requisite if you will. How and what you choose will make all the difference to your success as an interdependent human being, capable of creating wondrous synergies. These synergies will add value to your life, the lives of those around you, and hopefully to humanity. You'll come to find support and guidance from the TetraMap. It can help you in your personal development as well as guide you in developing others and the business that you are in.

The TetraMap® of Behavior

The TetraMap is liberating for those who grasp how Nature's basic elements, Earth, Air, Water and Fire are metaphors for behavior. It helps us appreciate what others bring to a situation, and to respect their natural behavior.

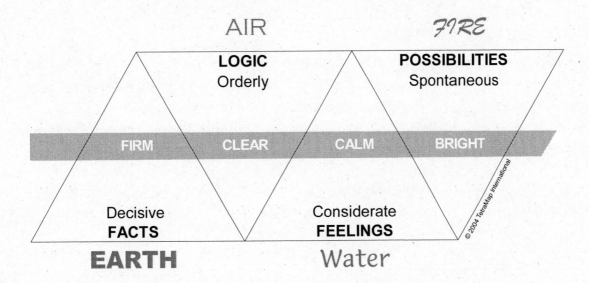

Note that *all* of us have *all* aspects of *all* of the four Elements, just in varying degrees. We each have different preferences, and some of these preferences may change under different situations, for example:

○ at work or at home

○ with role changes - becoming a coach/manager/leader/parent

○ under stress

TetraMap® Premises

○ Nature is a rich, cross-cultural metaphor.

○ Any complex system can be viewed from at least 4 different perspectives.

○ Multiple perspectives add depth and meaning.

What is the TetraMap® Used For?

Develop people and business the way Nature intended. It reminds us to:

○ Respect diversity.

○ Assume interdependency.

○ Take Responsibility.

The Map is Not the Territory

A map of the world shows latitude and longitude, but these lines are not actually etched onto the planet. Latitude and longitude are logical constructs that we use to divide this huge concept into pieces that we can understand. Similarly, the TetraMap divides *behavior* into elements that we can understand. The divisions exist only in the eye of the beholder.

There is no such thing as an Earth Element person... a Water Element person... We all have different combinations of each Element and the TetraMap merely gives us four perspectives of *how* we are different.

> *Seek similarities to distinguish the differences.*
> Yodimi

Do You Know These People?

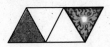 **External Focus** (Earth & Fire)
Act quickly, interested in outcomes.
Focus on affecting others' behavior.

 **Internal Focus** (Air & Water)
Think before acting, interested in process.
Focus on affecting own behavior.

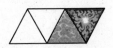 **Left-Brain** (Earth & Air)
Natural with numbers, languages and logic.
Task oriented, good at organizing others.

 **Right-Brain** (Water & Fire)
Natural with patterns, color and intuition.
People oriented, good at enrolling others.

 **Abstract/Conceptual Base** (Air & Fire)
Known for their up in the air ideas, theories and perceptions.

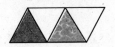 **Concrete/Practical Base** (Earth & Water)
Known for their down-to-earth deeds and common sense.

Behavioral Descriptions

Comparing ourselves to others of the same Element usually just confirms that everyone is different! The TetraMap is most useful in understanding how we are different to the other Elements. We begin to see characteristic patterns of behavior in others that indicate how we can modify our own behavior for better communication.

Earth, like a mountain, is often firm.
Big, bold and sturdy, Earth Elements are often leaders in the way they walk, talk and in the confident way they present themselves. Control, achievement and success are important, therefore quick, possibly risky decisions come easy.

Air, like the wind, is often clear.
These conscientious and focused individuals rely on their intellect and precision. Being critical thinkers, they excel in seeing the logic and rationale behind issues. Air Elements listen and plan to ensure accuracy and quality.

Water, like a lake, is often calm.
Caring and consistent, Water Elements are the foundations of families, teams and organizations. They are the loyal, deeply feeling people who show steadfast effort, great patience and a desire for harmony and flow.

Fire, like the sun, is often bright.
The eternal optimists, they love to see the possibilities and the brightness of the future. Fire Elements are often colorful and inspiring and have a great sense of fun!

Comparisons with Other Models

The TetraMap of Behavior is a compilation of researched work, spiritual teachings and direct experience with individuals, teams and entire organizations. It adds a new dimension to the four-quadrant representation of behavioral modes that has been with us for thousands of years.

2000   BRETTS' TETRAMAP® OF BEHAVIOR

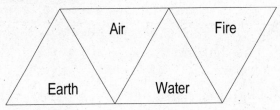

450 BC   HIPPOCRATES' FOUR HUMORS

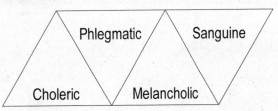

1923   JUNG'S PSYCHOLOGICAL TYPES

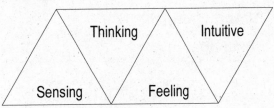

1928   MARSTON'S DISC MODEL

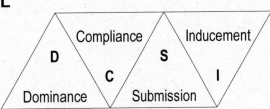

Hippocrates' Four Humors

The early Greek philosophers believed that everything in nature was made from four basic constituents, earth, air, water and fire. Hippocrates associated the four Elements with four different kinds of body fluids or *Humors*. He believed that the health, illnesses and temperament of each person depended on the relative balance of these Humors. These Temperaments correlate well with the behaviors of the TetraMap Elements, although the TetraMap and Greek Elements do not necessarily correspond. However, the Temperaments are assumed to be inherited, where the TetraMap assumes behavior is the result of interdependent preferences, both inherited and learned.

In modern times, Rudolf Steiner, the Austrian philosopher and educator taught teachers to recognize the four Temperaments in their students and to adapt to each individual's educational and emotional needs.

Jung's Psychological Types

Jung differentiates three dimensions or axes similar to the TetraMap:

TetraMap	Psychological Types
Internal Focus/External Focus	Introversion/Extroversion (attitude)
Practical/Conceptual	Sensing/Intuitive (irrational functions)
Left-Brain/Right-Brain	Thinking/Feeling (rational functions)

Jung's Types are based around a person's primary tendency towards one of the four functions, Sensing/Intuitive/Thinking/Feeling, plus the influence of attitude, either Introversion or Extroversion.

The TetraMap Elements would be interpreted:

TetraMap	Psychological Types
Earth	Extroverted Sensing
Air	Introverted Thinking
Water	Introverted Feeling
Fire	Extroverted Intuitive

Marston's DISC Model

In his book entitled *The Emotions of Normal People* Marston held that behavior depends on whether people are either active or passive and whether they perceive the environment to be favorable or unfavorable. This leads to Marston's four types:

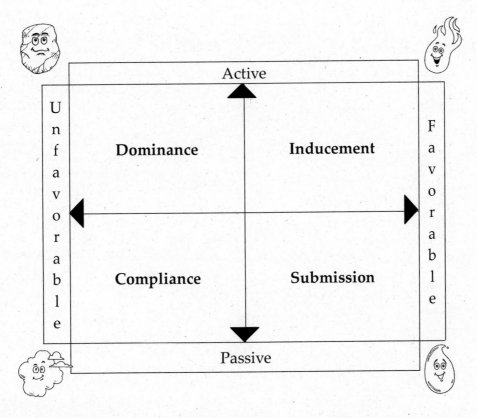

The terminology of the TetraMap is more neutral while characterizing much the same behavior.

Myers-Briggs Type Indicator (MBTI)

The MBTI measures preferences in terms of four independent axes of opposites – Introversion/Extroversion, Sensing/iNtuitive, Thinking/Feeling, Judgement/Perception. The TetraMap has a very different orientation – there are no opposites, and **inter-**dependence is emphasized. Effectively, the MBTI excels at showing how an individual is innately special, while the TetraMap excels at showing how others' general preferences are different.

Evolution of the Model

Chapter Overview

- Early Influences
- Discovering the Tetrahedron
- TetraMap Success Stories
- A Return to Holistic Thinking

Early Influences

Creating a metaphorical model of the world was not merely a passing thought or a concept derived from a wistful look at Nature. Its history is a fascinating sequence of events that started for us, Yoshimi and Jon Brett, in 1980.

Just prior to our return to New Zealand, we had just completed an adventure that included 8 months on the Pacific Ocean in a 32 foot ferro-cement yacht, 2 years living in Japan and our wedding in San Diego, California. The next stage of our adventure found us back in Auckland, New Zealand, Jon's birthplace as a genuine Kiwi from Down Under.

It was during the subsequent two years that we learned about the Four Elements, Earth, Air, Water and Fire. These were presented as a metaphorical, metaphysical understanding handed down from eons of time gone past. The *Elements of Man*, as they were referred to, were part of a philosophy that transcended time and standard generations of storytelling. The stories and lesson, in fact, were shared through a medium who channeled the ancient wisdom of an old Chinese man. This wise Chinese understood the nature of human nature and shared what we might learn from the metaphors of Earth, Air, Water and Fire.

With my background in education, and Jon's in biochemistry, we found conversations about the Elements questionable, but definitely intriguing. The four Elemental aspects of nature were discussed as if individuals reflected certain attributes linked to these elements: Earth: firm, bold, direct, decisive, confident people. Air: clear, logical, sequential, rational people. Water: calm, caring, sensitive, feeling people. Fire: bright, animated, optimistic, fun people.

Having little experience with other behavioral or personality models, the *Elements of Man* as taught to us by our friends, was a fascinating journey that spanned three years. Its significance hovered around the premise that such teachings would help us deal with people, and life in general, a bit better. The Elements were, so to speak, our initiation into the world of personal development. As we started to embrace the concept of Elemental preferences found in Earth, Air, Water and Fire, we also began to see how this information could help us to also understand why people behave the way they do. At this early stage, however, application remained a simple, fun, non-toxic way of viewing people and the world. The experience was not taken too seriously at the time, but in the big picture of our lives, it was one of the keys to our development and success as partners, facilitators and developers of the TetraMap.

In 1983, literature and tapes surrounding this study of the Elements were shelved. Both of us went head first into a new paradigm... business. Mystical in its own right, the realms of business also proved exciting though far more challenging. Throughout the subsequent years, we followed different paths as staff employees, free-lancers, managers and employers. Every now and then, we'd confer about office-life in relation to the Elements. Probably the best application of the knowledge around Earth, Air, Water, Fire still resided in understanding why and how people behaved to create the cultures they worked in.

In the early 1980's, the concepts of teamwork, organizational development and valuing human resources were still shallow, and in many places non-existent in New Zealand and Australia. Little was spoken about personal development, and seldom even mentioned in the same breath as work or business success. Both of us were fortunate to work within environmentally and socially enlightened organizations in both Australia and NZ throughout the rest of the '80's. These experiences fed our insight into the dynamics of functional teamwork and holistic work cultures, though they were certainly never labeled as such.

It was in the 1990's that I, Yoshimi, took another step 'into the mist' with my fourth retirement party. What next? Well, by now it was very clear that this Fire/Water Element thrived on change. What better way to move on than to combine the two work passions in my life… education and business? Blend these with personal development and you have a Fire Element's dream come true.

Imagine speaking to a room full of people…most of them actually listening and learning! This was my new career and was I in my element? Definitely! I'd officially entered the realms of facilitation and presentation, printed new business cards and set up shop. Based on successes as a GM- Operations that allowed me to focus on teamwork, customer service and organizational development, I was invited to work with teams, large and small, from senior management to factory floor.

It was in this environment that the Four Elements made a comeback into our lives. For years, conversations about Earth, Air, Water and Fire were held between us and a few friends who shared similar lessons or who were directly involved in the original teachings. Because the information was received via, let's say unscientific and boldly metaphysical means, discussion and applications were limited to our own understanding of the universe. Now, with some experience under our belts with regard to human resource development in a business context, we were able to expand our understandings and venture forward to learn more specifically about what drives people in the workplace to work together… or not.

The Four Elements meet DISC

In 1991, DISC and the work of Marston entered our lives during a personal development course. The standard multiple choice questionnaire and ensuing pages of text were fascinating but quite inwardly focused. It was wonderful to learn about self, appropriate career paths for our personality types, but this information did not support our communication skills and relationships.

The Elements, however, were all there between the lines and columns of the DISC profile. What we'd learned years ago about Earth, Air, Water, Fire integrated nicely. Overlaying the Elements over the DISC model, the distinctions became obvious. The business world had an interesting and very successful model in DISC, but the Elements seemed more intuitively satisfying.

The typical four-quadrant approach to categorizing personalities fitted in well with models we'd studied - Hippocrates, Jung, Herrmann and a multitude of others. The four-quadrant framework was popular and easy for making comparisons. There's the famous Myers-Briggs with its many letters and extensive research. Ned Herrmann's four quadrant brain-dominance model was particularly interesting. We had the good fortune of hearing him in person at an Accelerated Learning Conference in the USA. Ned's voice, manner, confidence, vocabulary and entire presence exuded an Earth/Air preference. He was emphatic about the need for the learning community to be more research and evidence focused in its assumptions about learning.

Most of these models had extensive backdrops of research, examination and statistics. Many required an entire course just to explain them, let alone be certified to explain them to someone else. Meanwhile, the facilitation work that I chose was learner-focused. It was meant to be fun, fast, and inspire action. If one couldn't easily remember the meaning of being an ENFP, not to mention what the letters stood for, how could the information be passed on easily?

It was back to Nature for Jon and me so that by the mid 90's, we decided to team up and create our own facilitation services company. We returned to the four Elements that were still in their comfortable four-quadrant form with Earth and

Water sitting opposite each other, and Air and Fire also in juxtapose positions. Visually, it was a wonderful model with each natural Element portrayed by a geometric face shape.

Dave Gunson, artist, did a wonderful job of depicting those four face shapes and Elemental qualities in a logo that was both functional and aesthetically beautiful. However, it turned out that relating the Elements to face shapes was not part of the original teachings. They were developed independently, therefore inappropriate to share in our work. We were forced to find a new way of presenting Earth, Air, Water and Fire.

This was a major setback, but by this time in our lives we'd learned that disappointments were often catalysts and opportunities for change. As the left-brained, kinesthetic genius of the family, Jon stepped up to the challenge with ease and grace... and a lot of help from the great work of Buckminster Fuller.

Through all these years of developing and integrating the four Elements of Nature into our work, the writings of Buckminster Fuller have been the most influential and credible. Bucky was one of the few men in history who physically and mathematically demonstrated his ideas. Though difficult to decipher, his writing is filled with logic, meaning and solutions.

Understanding models should not be rocket science, particularly if they are created to support personal or organizational success. Our model based on the four Elements of Nature simplified understanding of self and others.

The subsequent years of development that involved redesigning and placement of the Elements onto Bucky's *minimum structural system in Universe*, the tetrahedron, became our life's work. The Four Elements Tetrahedron model (a real mouthful to say and perhaps comprehend) eventually developed into a simple map! Unfolding the tetrahedron became a TetraMap. Born in the new millennium, the TetraMap has since become a powerful guide for not only the behavioral understandings it presents, but for its application to the logic behind our holistic world and way of thinking.

Discovering the Tetrahedron

During the 90s, we were introduced to the wisdom of R. Buckminster Fuller (or *Bucky*, as he is often called). An American who died in 1983, he is probably best known for his geodesic dome architectural design, and his books, *Critical Path* and *Operating Manual for Spaceship Earth*. Rather than being a specialist, he called himself a comprehensivist, making significant contributions in the areas of architecture, physics, mathematics, numerology, philosophy, religion, art, literature, naturalism, urban development, industry, and technology. Quite a guy! Controversial too.

In his 1975 book, *Synergetics*, Bucky asserts:

> *Synergetics shows how we may measure our experiences geometrically and topologically and how we may employ geometry and topology to coordinate all information regarding our experiences, both metaphysical and physical.*

Bucky had this thing about the tetrahedron, and was scathing about cubes. He describes the tetrahedron as *the minimum structural system in Universe*. In his posthumously published book, *Cosmography*, he elaborates (page 41):

We wonder how it can be that nature develops a virus or the billions of beautiful bubbles in the wake of a ship. How does she formulate these lovely geometries so rapidly? She must have some fundamental, simple, and pure way of developing these extraordinary life cells and chemistries.

I discovered that the tetrahedron was at the root of the matter.

© 2004 TetraMap International

Could the tetrahedron be at the root of natural human behavior? Why is it that so many accepted models of behavior are based around *four* main types? Could the physical properties of the tetrahedron reflect four different aspects of behavior?

What, No Opposites?

The most intriguing property of a tetrahedron is that it has no opposites.

○ No two sides are opposite.

○ No two vertices are opposite.

Our brains love opposites, so the tetrahedron is really rather disappointing in that respect. No wonder we have so little use for this geometric shape. The cube on the other hand is loaded with opposites - we often *put people in boxes* in order to understand them better. Usually this is not very popular. Perhaps the tetrahedron provides us with a clue as to why we naturally feel uncomfortable being *pigeon holed*. Perhaps opposites are sometimes just an illusion fabricated by our brains to make sense of diversity. Perhaps the tetrahedron holds the secret to understanding diversity.

There is a satisfying sense of symmetry in the tetrahedron.

○ Each face is the same size and shape.

○ Each edge is exactly the same length.

○ Each face adjoins all the other faces.

There is a sense of equality and being interconnected. Is this just a geometric shape we are talking about? *Equal and interconnected* - we could be talking about human beings. Perhaps Bucky is right, and the tetrahedron really is *at the root of the matter*.

Depicting the Tetrahedron

But how do you put a tetrahedron in a book? This simple shape is difficult to visualize on a flat piece of paper. When we label all four sides, at least one side is always hidden behind the others.

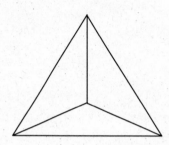

Obviously we had to unfold the tetrahedron into some logical arrangement of four triangles.

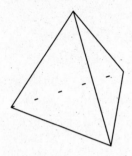

Opening out the tetrahedron like a box had a nice symmetry about it, but the central triangle was too special, too different to the others.

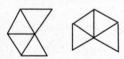

This shape had some promise, but doesn't actually fold into the tetrahedron - two faces overlap.

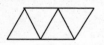

It had to be four triangles in a row, but how should we map the Elements of natural human behavior onto them?

Up/Down

Earth and Water are more affected by gravity and tend to fall down. Let's put them in the triangles with their bases down. Air and Fire tend to float up, so they go in the triangles with their bases at the top. This is consistent with our understanding of human behavior:

 UP is **abstract, conceptual** – like when you look up to visualize or imagine something. Air behavior is characterized by thinking, analyzing, theorizing. Fire behavior is typically imaginative.

 DOWN is **concrete, practical** - like when you have your feet on the ground and look downward to remember what something felt like. Earth behavior tends to be aiming at tangible results. Feelings are a Water specialty. Water behavior seeks the path of least resistance, hoping to avoid conflict.

An example of this up-down relationship is apparent in any business or corporation. The larger the business, the more opportunity… and challenge… in creating synergistic outcomes. Take the Sales, Finance, Service and Marketing functions within an organization. Often working in silos with a, *we're the center of the universe* mentality coming from each, many organizations work with distinct departments of endeavor.

The up side of the organization is:

○ Fire - Marketing's creative concepts and communication skills, which inspire the customer to buy.

○ Air - Finance and Technology's contribution to the organization's systems.

Meanwhile, at ground level, Earth and Water beaver away at the *doing* side of Sales and Service. Far more practical and down-to-earth, both Earth and Water are at the coalface dealing with customers.

Left/Right

Earth and Air behavior is more **left-brained** – natural with numbers, languages and logic. It is also more **task-oriented**, good at organizing others.

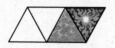
Water and Fire behavior is more **right-brained** – natural with patterns, color and intuition. It is also more **people-oriented**, good at enrolling others.

Left-brain, right-brain theory has become wide spread. Here's a quick overview of research which has shown the capacities governed by each hemisphere of the brain.

Left-Brain	Right-Brain
Numbers	Emotion
Linear	Random
Words	Pictures
Analytical thinking	Global thinking
Sequence	Patterns
Literal	Metaphors
Evidence	Intuition

Earth and Air tend to be more left-brained, Water and Fire, more right-brained. This is demonstrated daily as we see those who are task-focused, finding solutions, and getting things done - be it building something, reporting, gathering and interpreting information, doing, doing, doing.

In the meantime, Water and Fire are busy being with others - communicating, discussing, listening, networking, caring and inspiring.

It was particularly obvious at a workshop for a well-known clothing designer and manufacturer. A presentation was made by the Sales Manager and Marketing

Manager, both of whom scored highest as Fire Elements. The question they were addressing was *What motivates you and keeps you motivated under pressure?*

Basically the Fire in each of these people was high. They loved people, networking, fun and new ideas. Their presentation together was colorful and entertaining. The difference was dramatically demonstrated as they each took center stage to present their answer to the second part of the question. The Sales Manager spoke of the need to be supported, valued and the responsibility felt for the well being of others. Water was surfacing quickly.

The Marketing Manager boldly stated that achievement and results maintained momentum. Reaching of goals and targets was the motivation. Earth was thrusting into view.

There was a balance there, in behavior as well as in leading the Sales and Marketing departments. The strength and natural preference of each Manager balanced the need for people-care as well as results. Synergy happened in this company... naturally.

Internal/External △▽△▽

 Earth and Fire behavior is more **externally focused** – interested in **outcomes** and affecting others' behavior.

 Air and Water behavior is more **internally focused** – interested in **process** and affecting their own behavior.

We always get a knowing chuckle when this TetraMap configuration is described. Earth and Fire are *out there*. Pushing and pulling for attention, results and control. Usually excellent communicators, these externally focused people either *lay it on the line* or help others to see the dream. Either way, Earth and Fire get the message across.

Air and Water provide refreshment, as they tend to think before speaking. More internal in nature, analysis, reflection and contemplation are in order before putting forward thoughts. Sometimes having difficulty expressing themselves, Air and Water often choose the listening pose...allowing Earth and Fire to be in their Element as externally focused communicators.

A husband and wife team comes to mind. A fun, task-oriented Fire and Earth husband forms a business as well as marriage team with a lovely, quiet, soft-spoken Water and Air partner. Their roles at home and work mirror their Elemental preferences beautifully.

Sales, marketing, public speaking...even a toe in the political scene keeps the Fire/Earth active. The need for freedom is often high on the values list for Fire, thus the entrepreneurial spirit abounds. The combination of Fire and Earth are great for these independent individuals who would find the confines of working for someone else far too claustrophobic.

On the other hand, the Water/Air partner does what? Office administration of course. More importantly, she's perfect for the job of keeping the externally focused M.D. (sometimes standing for Mad Director) in line both at home and in the office. Softly, with compassion she maintains a sense of balance, harmony and family-values in the office.

This external and internal pull-push demonstrates an excellent balance for this couple and business, which is healthy, alive and developing.

In/Out Energy

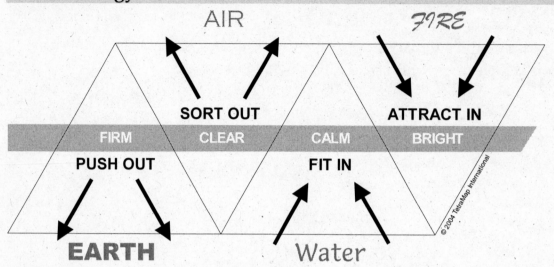

 EARTH: **PUSH OUT (DIVERGING)**

Mountains thrust out of the ground. Energy is pushed out with the intention of action and tangible achievement.

 AIR: **SORT OUT (DIVERGING)**

Wind separates the wheat from the chaff. Energy is pushed out, with the intention of discarding what is not wanted, and sorting out what is.

 WATER: **FIT IN (CONVERGING)**

A river gathers water from many different streams and mixes it together. Energy is pulled inwards with the intention of fitting in and converging towards unity.

 FIRE: **ATTRACT IN (CONVERGING)**

A warm fire glows invitingly. Energy is attracted in with the intention of creating an impression.

Logical Integrity

All this symmetry gives the model a surprising logical integrity. The intuitive simplicity is astonishing, and one can't help but wonder if perhaps there is more logic yet to be discovered!

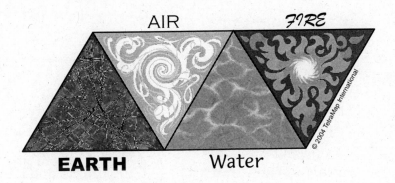

The Map is Not the Territory

Fold the TetraMap back up into a tetrahedron, and suddenly the wonderful symmetry disappears! Where are the left and right faces? There is no left/right. There is no up/down. At first this seems to be a setback, but it really just adds an intriguing twist. The TetraMap is just a map, a representation of reality. It is not the real thing.

Elemental Balance

Many self-development books strive to help us answer the question:
What if I could unleash the power within me to lead the life I choose? Would I be a balanced individual and would my natural Earth, Air, Water and Fire behaviors express themselves fully?

If we look at life as a TetraMap, perhaps the following questions and affirmations will ensure balance:

○ **Earth is Firm**. Am I firm in my goals?
I am firm, determined and focused in my goals, be they financial, work achievement, family, community or health. I take action each day toward achieving those goals and am strong, able and fit in mind and body to do so.

○ **Air is Clear**. Am I clear in my knowledge?
I am clear about what I need to know and have a strategy for learning. Every day is a learning day to improve myself, my life and to add value to those around me.

○ **Water is Calm**. Am I calm in my relationships with others?
I have calm compassion for family, friends and humanity. I am caring and supportive of myself and of my relationships.

○ **Fire is Bright**. Am I bright in expressing my vision for the future?
I am bright and optimistic about the future and how I can contribute to that future. I inspire myself and others to live to our full potential and leave legacies that make a positive difference.

The TetraMap gives us a tool to look at almost anything from four different perspectives. It is a tool to chunk down complexity in a holistic way, enabling more balance in our solutions, assessments and actions.

TetraMap® Success Stories

As a new millennium model, the TetraMap's history is short. However, the years preceding 2000 were filled with development, experimentation, successes and lots and lots of learning. The greatest satisfaction was in the success of the TetraMap in achieving its original goals:

❍ Provide a fun, inexpensive tool for clients to use for self-discovery and to learn about others.

❍ Simplify and demystify personality typing by using an easy to remember and powerful metaphor, Nature.

❍ Support positive communication and relationship building.

❍ Help clients to embrace and respect diversity and thereby strengthen team performance.

The following stories are, a fascinating recollections of how the TetraMap, or in the early days, *The Four Elements Tetrahedron Model* have added value to individuals, teams and whole organizations.

Why Are You Like That?

In the early days of TetraMap development, we shyly slipped the four Elements into a training session, introducing it as an icebreaker or quick get-to-know-each-other activity called *Why Are You Like That?* Never presuming it would replace other personality models used in the corporate environment, we believed that making the small difference that it did was enough.

> *After using other behavioral instruments for a number of years, I've found that the model has added excellent value to our training and consultancy business. We now use the Why Are You Like That? Workbooks. It is well received and aids in changing perceptions, attitudes and behaviors.*
>
> V. Jackson, Director, Trainer, Wellington, New Zealand

More recently, feedback and visible, tangible results have given us confidence that the TetraMap warrants a place in many Human Resources and Organizational Development programs. As the metaphor of Nature becomes more meaningful and the integrity of the model extends beyond behavior to a systems thinking approach to organizational issues, the TetraMap has come to stand on its own. Research and data gathering are happening, but in the meantime, there's no excuse for waiting. The TetraMap is about doing something now to improve communication, to explore new perspectives and to find holistic solutions to personal, workplace, community and global challenges.

I was on a personal visit to Washington DC these past few days and serendipitously was exposed to a new self evaluation tool which seems far more effective than MBTI, True Colors, etc. It is simpler to use by both the individual and the facilitator, and is quite inexpensive. The first order results are instantaneously effective and can be applied in any scenario, meeting, class, etc.; in fact any circumstance involving human interaction.

T. Pattinson, Director, Words-A-Way, Quebec, Canada

I have had great fun with the elements. I have taken Myers-Briggs and other personality tests, but the elements are the easiest to relate to real life.

M. Hock, Webmaster, Alexandria, Virginia.

In my training with people from all walks of life - corporate, non-corporate and young people - I have found the Why Are You Like That? Process to be very easy to use. After trialing the package, Scouting New Zealand has now incorporated it into their Advanced Leader Training Program, replacing an existing behavioral model. [The TetraMap] is a fresh approach to introducing behavioral characteristics and its strength is in the value placed in people's uniqueness.

J. Williams, Director, Trainer, Wellington, New Zealand

> *I am now shocked at how in-tune with my values and personality I am. Coming from a Psychology studies background, I approached this TetraMap ideology with more than the proverbial grain of salt. I found that the exercises led to great clarity and understanding of my nature which can be placed into any individual or teamwork context. Big ups!*
>
> C. Brown, Student, Victoria University of Wellington, NZ

In-House Organizational Communication

> *I want you to know that since we met last summer I have been using the Why Are You Like That? Workbook on a pretty informal basis with co-workers, friends and family. I had them out at a social gathering a few weeks ago with friends I have known for years. It was great and I learned a lot. I have used it with all the people in my department at work and with my daughter. The insight is quick and profound.*
>
> *As I said I have kept this informal at work because I am a supervisor and didn't want anyone to feel required to take it. Everyone learned something and I am better able to communicate now. I understand my daughter's actions because of her high earth. I used it one time with people before a workshop started. Sure did understand my audience better!! I have especially liked using it with young people--they love it and "get it" really fast!*
>
> M. Hartson, Training Director, Mother, Hyattsville, Maryland

This letter arrived the season after we had introduced the TetraMap in Mexico City at an Accelerated Learning Conference. Obviously something struck a cord with her and she embraced its potential.

The key learning here is the ease with which the four Elements are understood. The four Elements of Nature, Earth, Air, Water and Fire immediately bring to mind intuitive understandings of the metaphor. It is easy to consider an Earthy, firm, hands-on person, an Airy, clear thinking person, a Watery, calm and caring person, and a Fiery, optimistic and bright person.

In her role as Training Director of a large organization, she has since used the TetraMap of Behavior to help staff members achieve the following.

- Understand each other's preferences, needs and motives better.
- Find a common language that focuses on the positive attributes of individuals and how outcomes can be achieved by recognizing these preferences.

We have since had the privilege of working with this organization and meeting its talented and dedicated people . After facilitating the *Why Are You Like That?* process, we were preparing for a different workshop on day 2 when a participant from the previous day popped in to say hello.

She was bubbling with enthusiasm as she described a meeting she'd had with her manager after the *Why Are You Like That?* session. It seems she'd had an enlightening and memorable experience describing the Elements and explaining to her boss her natural preferences. It was an eye-opener for both to find that they had so blatantly misinterpreted each other. The discussion was revealing and made all the difference to their relationship from that point forward.

Needless to say, this organization has been touched by the TetraMap and has embraced an exciting way of viewing the world and each other.

Following are more messages from the Training Director and a Manager from the same organization.

The TetraMap of Behavior has brought results beyond my expectations. Employees have found a new way of communicating because they have had a personal experience with The Elements. People use the information they learned to talk about differences and similarities, to conduct meetings more effectively and to talk through staff evaluations.

I have been amazed by the power of this tool. I cannot recommend it strongly enough to any company who wants its workforce to improve communication on a daily basis. We have a new language!

M. Hartson, Training Director, Columbia, Maryland

Yoshimi and Jon brought an amazingly easy, yet powerful tool into our business culture. The presentation by Yoshimi of these ideas was so clear that there was an instant recognition and an "a-ha!" within the group. We've actually begun to communicate on a daily basis using these elements and all that they mean.

D. Hart, Director of Online Services, Columbia, Maryland

Personal and Team Transformation

Team-building sessions are often transformational. Because high performance teamwork requires focus, self-sacrifice and very high trust amongst team members, the exercises and processes involved are challenging and require stretch.

The TetraMap makes the stretch of considering multiple perspectives, a bit easier to understand and digest. The process of discovering individual preferences is always fun, and debriefing and discussing what this means can open new paradigms of thought for many.

TetraMap is one of the greatest inventions because it shows that none of us is perfect, but it also demonstrates that we can achieve perfection by working together.

M. Sedoglavic, Student, Waikato University, NZ

> *[The workshop] successfully stripped a team of 30 or so recruitment consultants of their self-destroying egos and reminded us what we are made of and what our strengths and weaknesses are. Rather than questioning why people don't think and behave as I do, I now realize that our differences in the workplace are just as, if not more important than our similarities. I have a greater understanding of my personal relationships because of the theory you introduced us to.*
>
> L. Sheldon, Personnel Consultant, Melbourne, Australia

Inviting people to share their own Earth, Air, Water, or Fire preferences is enjoyable. Asking them to celebrate these same attributes in others is more of a challenge. In team building, or in fact, in any relationship building situation, accepting the 'weakness' of others is vital. The first paradigm to break is that this so-called weakness, may be a strength that is simply misplaced, misaligned or mistimed.

> *I found the four Elements of Earth, Air, Water, and Fire to be very useful categories when trying to look at the way a person or a group of people is behaving at a holistic level. I realized that certain qualities of the Elements that I had previously had absolutely no personal connection to, are not bad qualities but are in fact essential to productive behavior. I realized that all the four Elements complement each other and can help you become a more balanced person.*
>
> R. Mercer, Student, Victoria University of Wellington, NZ

> *It made me see all the personalities/qualities as positive and interdependent. Before hand I'd sometimes feel intimidated by more spontaneous, bossy (i.e. Fire & Earth) people but now I've come to understand it all more. It's been so great because I feel I will understand and consider people more now. Also it was comforting to meet people similar to me and realizing how comfortable it was to be around Water and Air people, yet a bit unproductive.* Anonymous

Building relationships is a challenging exercise in itself, whether in a team, the workplace, the home or the community. When you think of it, relationship building is a daily exercise. When we focus on specific skills to improve communication and relationships, the TetraMap comes in handy as a map based in something we are already familiar with... Nature. The transition from the TetraMap of Nature to the TetraMap of Behavior is easy and painless. The map makes sense.

> *The TetraMap has given me a clearer framework from which to more easily identify the working style of others and how to work with those people.*
>
> S. Bennet, Student, Victoria University of Wellington, NZ

However, we must constantly remind ourselves that the map is not the territory. The map is not reality, but it can help us to see ourselves in a different light with a sense of dignity, celebration and even fun. Understanding skills and techniques to improve communication in the workplace can often be a powerful catalyst to embracing a new way of seeing and behaving in the world.

> *The TetraMap is a simple, easy to understand concept that can be used at any level within our organization from managers through to manufacturing. Using the TetraMap to explain and work through peoples behaviors has enabled us to develop teams into productive, motivated groups that understand, communicate and support each other in order to achieve the goals of the group and the company.*
>
> G. Nathan, Employee Development Officer, Auckland, New Zealand

A bit of instant feedback...
Just to let you know - I ran a session today with a small customer services team (6 people) - the team had all the elements in it, which was great. Outcome: a real appreciation for the other elements and also realizations that they were incredibly adaptable and able to think, act...communicate with elements completely different to them. I'll definitely use this again.

J. Waldman, Training Manager, Auckland, New Zealand

I recently purchased the Why Are You Like That? *training pack and have used it with great success in our business. The concepts are simple and easy to relate to and are already starting to improve communication within teams.*

L. Sparrow, Manager, Sydney, Australia

Strategic Planning

The use of the TetraMap sets a firm foundation as an opening process for a number of organizational development challenges. One of the more recent and exciting applications has been the TetraMap's role in strategic planning, (as described in *Visionary Team Planning Process*, page 107).

Having extensively studied strategic management and developing strategic plans, I have to say I was profoundly surprised by the new dimension that [the TetraMap] can bring to a strategic development process.

T. Hall, CEO, South Taranaki, New Zealand

We've supported the strategic planning process for a variety of organizations large and small. From very systematic, model-based formats, to more free-wheeling visioning sessions and everything in between, the chosen design of the planning process reflects the nature of the organization.

In earlier sessions at either end of the planning spectrum, there always seemed to be something missing. Sometimes it was a lack of vision clarity… often times it was confusion or lack of buy-in from management or staff. Other times a fantastic, compelling vision was left to burn brightly with no tangible plan of action. In contrast, other sessions resulted in wonderful action plans with little to no accountability for seeing the actions through or no clear cut way of deciphering if and when the targets were actually achieved.

The TetraMap again provided evidence that a holistic perspective is not only natural, but also comprehensive. Working with 12 -24 people often ensures that all areas of the organization are contributing. No longer is the visioning process limited to the thoughts of a few at the top. The process instead focuses on:

○   A cross representation of the group that the plan is intended to guide.

○   People contribute from perspectives that reflect their natural motives and interests.

○   At minimum, four perspectives encompass a holistic approach to planning and action taking.

> *I was very pleased that we were able to use the 4 Elements to help the team understand each other in simple and uncomplicated ways. Subsequently assigning the Elements with roles and actions for our business development that aligned with their nature has had huge tangible benefits already.*
>
> G. Simpson, General Manager, Auckland, New Zealand

Training Consultants

Trainers, facilitators, consultants and human resource managers have incredible choice in terms of finding product solutions to their organizational training issues. Each solution reflects a personality of its own and undoubtedly mirrors the background and intent of its author. The TetraMap is no different as it quickly appeals to Fire and Water Elements. Earth Elements realize the value of the model through tangible experience and observations. Air Elements may find the model a bit lightweight until the integrity and logic of the TetraMap become apparent.

Trainers, managers and educators who embrace the beauty and logic of the model and who support the success of their learners, find the TetraMap to be a rich, meaningful and useful map. Not only does the TetraMap serve as a guide to improving relationships, but also provides a holistic perspective on people and business development.

> My experience is that people love to learn more about themselves, and in your friendly and open forum, they **do** learn about themselves. More importantly in the team building process, having learned about and accepted themselves, they are far more accepting of the diversity of others.
>
> J. Davies, Director, Trainer, Christchurch, New Zealand

> Our team of facilitators has used the TetraMap in training, development and coaching for a diverse range of clients. It is applicable for teambuilding, customer service, people management, conflict resolution and any other situation where communication and relationship building has value.
>
> J. Alley, Director, Trainer, Auckland, New Zealand

> We had a fun time - the feedback was great. During the debrief, the learnings came through really well. I'm hearing this morning many people being a lot more careful about how they approach their communication with each other. This is an area that needed improving! I used the above as a lead into a change management workshop.
>
> M. Louie, Training Consultant, Auckland, New Zealand

Students

The TetraMap, as a new millennium model, will hopefully find its place with the leaders of tomorrow. Presented for over 4 years as a tool for newly enrolled MBA students, the concept has also found popularity with University undergraduates. The simplicity and sheer delight of learning about self and others gets energetic, optimistic responses from our leaders of tomorrow.

> *Wow, you guys rock. It was excellent to be able to identify my "style" and what I need to work on to be able to make myself more well rounded and able to work in a team environment.* Anonymous University Under-graduate

> *TetraMap - an awesome eye-opener bringing a concise and highly logical technique in classifying personality types and suitable learning techniques (personality dependent & learning dependent) for what would beforehand have seemed a daunting task.*
>
> E. Hung, Student, Waikato University, New Zealand

> *The TetraMap concept really helped me understand the perspectives of my team members and how we can work together better as a team.*
>
> F. Macdonald, AIESEC Regional President, Auckland University, NZ

> *The TetraMap made me think about how all elements of personality type are present in each individual, and helped me identify the areas where I can step out of my comfort zone and develop myself to my full potential. It also made me think about interacting with different people and the importance of appreciating where others are coming from.*
>
> E. Raingford, Student, Victoria University of Wellington, New Zealand

> *The TetraMap helped me to understand how I tick, but more importantly, how others tick. It also helped me to see there is a little bit of Fire, Air, Water & Earth in all of us.*
>
> R. Hunter, Student, University of Otago, New Zealand

Primary & Secondary Preferences

It is helpful to remind ourselves that every one of us houses and demonstrates the behavioral preferences of all four Elements. It's also interesting to remember that many of us have two preferences that complement each other to create our uniqueness. Whether a person is an Earth/Fire, Air/Water, Water/Fire, Fire/Air, or any other combination, how each perceives and reacts to the world is a unique blend of the Elements in the circumstance of the moment.

Understanding Earth, Air, Water and Fire for their more common preferences however, can be of great help to any manager, leader, facilitator, parent or friend. The distinctions between a Water/Fire Element and a Water/Air Element can range from a small behavioral tendency to a substantial difference in motives and approach.

The following letter came from a manager who has come to understand the Elements through a variety of team and planning workshops. This manager has obviously tapped into the deeper benefits and value that the TetraMap offers.

> *I have recently bought together a new team of people within a large New Zealand company. Team members came from different places within the organization, and ranged in age from 25 to 53. They ranged in skill types from someone who was recently a customer service rep to someone who'd been responsible for running an IT shop with multi-million dollar budget responsibilities.*
>
> *I used the TetraMap exercise for our first-ever planning session as a team. The exercise had a triple purpose - as an exercise to help people relax and feel comfortable with each other, as a tool to gain greater understanding of each other, and as a tool to give me, as their manager, a greater understanding of "where they are coming from".*
>
> *Despite the variety of backgrounds and ages, the tool proved valuable for everyone, giving them greater understanding and placing them all on the same level irrespective of their place in the team or their age/experience.*

Whilst it was relatively easy to recognize people's first Element, the second provided a valuable guide to behavior. For instance, one person whose primary Element is Water felt very insecure about the role in the new team. The second Element, Air, gave me insight into why the person seem weighted with so many problems. The person's role was new and not detailed or numerated in terms of specific responsibilities and deliverables. The person felt that there weren't enough facts or clarity about what was expected. There was concern about how they were going to be measured (performance appraised). As Water, this person was very in touch with personal emotions which, as an Air Element, created incredible discomfort!!!

I would recommend the TetraMap as a great tool for all teams. We continue to use it to explain to each other why we have acted the way we have and how to help us do our jobs the best we can, particularly when the going gets tough".

T. Sutton, Program Director Operations, Wellington, New Zealand

A Return to Holistic Thinking

Twenty-two years down the track, the initial insights into the four Elements of Nature have gone to depths never imagined. As the key forces and elements of this planet Earth, these four Elements not only help us to describe our own nature, but the nature of almost everything that we see, do or touch.

Nature is holistic. Nature is synergistic. Nature is interdependent. Every movement, action, thought, behavior has an effect on something else. Many religions, cultures and models reflect this interaction, and yet as humans we continue to work in silos and believe, or care little for the effect we have on each other. We often overlook the opportunities for synergy and the possibilities of what we can create in an interdependent world.

As in the health and learning sectors of many cultures, the return to holism is apparent. Excruciatingly slow as the process may seem, there is an on-going search for holistic solutions to illness - physical, mental and emotional. There are persistent educational campaigns that consider the holistic view of the learning individual. Scientific studies into brain-based learning, psychoneuroimmunology (PNI) and a myriad of mind/body research support our holistic understanding.

It's amazing that so many cultures have lost touch with ancient and even more recent endeavors of holistic health and education. In man's efforts to modernize, globalize and profitize, many old-world solutions, remedies and concepts have been tossed out or ignored. Our ancestors had much to teach us. It's somehow disconcerting that we seem to have forgotten or choose to forget in the name of progress and growth.

In the meantime, the pace of new research is dauntingly slow and costly. Waiting is not an excuse for slowing down the forward thrust and development of what we do know, or remember. We do know that learning is no longer about input and output of data. We do know that people learn in a myriad of ways and that we as educators, parents, facilitators, trainers, managers and in general, responsible human beings, can better embrace diversity and differences if we also embrace holistic perspectives of the world.

There is no excuse for not working together synergistically. There is no excuse for silo mentality, whether it be in a corporation that houses four distinct departments called Sales, Marketing, Service and Finance, each believing that it holds the place together. Or a culture holding on to traditions of violence, hatred and superiority, believing that the actions they take have no repercussions on the sustainability of the planet and humankind.

Take a moment to consider again the four Elements within each of us. The firmness and stability of Earth, the clarity and all-knowingness of Air, the calm and compassion of Water, and the brightness and inspiration of Fire. The synergy of the four Elements in Nature creates beauty and life itself. The synergy of the four Elements in our nature allows us to create new synergies and far more than we could ever do independently.

Evolution of the Model

TetraMap - How to Develop People & Business the Way Nature Intended

Earth Air Water Fire

Chapter Summary

○ Recognizing the Elements

○ Approaching the Elements

○ Flexibility

○ The Elements of Teamwork

Recognizing the Elements

In our never-ending attempt to understand people and situations better, categorizations such as Achievers, Thinkers, Feelers or Innovators… or perhaps Choleric, Phlegmatic, Melancholic, or Sanguine may come into play. We might be asked whether we relate best to triangles, squares, circles or squiggles… or whether we were born a Taurus, Libra, Pisces, Sagittarius… Categorizing personality styles to better understand people is common and entertaining.

Recognizing each of the Elements in the real world is fascinating and can be a major part of personal development. It adds the responsibility to embrace diversity and to work for a better world. The responsibility involves respecting each Element's contribution. It involves not giving in to blaming others. It involves taking time to consider each Element's strengths first, then to tactfully flow in sync with the other person.

Beware of making assumptions - the TetraMap is a blunt instrument, like most behavioral models. Every individual is unique and complex. Our focus is not to categorize people, but to celebrate uniqueness while taking on the challenges involved in creating synergy.

As we better understand and recognize the Elements, we are also stepping-up to the challenges of making life work for everyone at both individual and group levels. Our responsibilities will expand to considering multiple perspectives… looking at life from the perspectives of Earth, Air, Water and Fire.

Vocabulary, Voice Tone and Body Language

You'll find that your personal strategies to deal with those you love, work and play will develop as you develop your alertness to the Elements. People display and speak their Elements all the time, it's just a matter of listening and watching.

Reading the snippets of conversations in this section will help you to recognize how each Element might approach a specific situation. Earth Elements will be direct, succinct, few on words and to the point. They tend to look the listener in the eye and be alert to whether what they are saying is being received and understood. Earth will not wait long for a response. An Earth voice tends to be just that, Earthy, deep and direct.

Remember that the second Element preference plays an important part. For instance an Earth/Fire Element may speak faster than and Earth/Air and have no problems in changing subjects quickly. Take this to the extreme of a very Fiery Fire, where you may feel you are being machine gunned with words. Be alert, as subject and focus may change in a heartbeat… and restart further down the track… and have a question tacked on at the end.

Fire are usually easy to recognize as their arms wave about to make their many points and their excitement is almost uncontainable. Intonation goes up, down, every which way to express themselves and to ensure every possible listener is looking their way.

Water and Air Elements in contrast tend to be far softer in approach and voice tone. Water, like a bubbling brook, sometimes mumble with eyes averted to avoid direct attention. To ensure that no offence is taken, Water often speaks slowly with pauses for thought. Often lengthy dissertations are required to explain all the considerations.

Similarly, though possibly more deliberately, Air Elements speak clearly, taking time to ensure correctness of speech and analysis of situations. With attention to detail and often, lengthy defining statements, Air will ensure that what is said is complete, accurate and provides evidence.

Look for All the Elements

Never lock anyone into a certain Element…even if you're sure. This includes you. We are human, we are complex, and we are diverse. The tetrahedron is a wonderful metaphor. It too is complex, it has an inside and an outside, it is a complete system, and it has no opposites. Unfold the tetrahedron to make a TetraMap and you have Earth, Air, Water, and Fire. Each one of us has the preferences of each of these Elements, though in varying degrees.

By being flexible, we can be assured that we do not lock ourselves or others into one, or even two Elements, but that we use the information to help us respond with more dignity, compassion and sense in our daily communication.

So let's begin by getting to know and recognizing the Elements! This is not about blaming someone for being a certain Element. It is about recognizing and acknowledging natural strengths, and blending them with your own nature for synergistic outcomes.

In the following sections, 'listen' carefully and you will learn. The first three scenarios start off with comments by Earth, Air, Water then Fire in that order. Hints follow to help you recognize specific characteristics. You get to practice recognizing the Elements from the fourth scenario on.

Enjoy! When you've finished reading, start really listening to those around you, their vocabulary, intonation, motivations and wants. Listen to understand. You'll soon come to recognize diverse strengths ways to build more positive, win/win outcomes!

Natural Preferences

 Get real. Get grounded. Want to know how you're doing? Look at your results.

 Thinking about this, it makes sense to take an orderly approach and check what the drawbacks are.

 Let's close our eyes and take a moment to relax and reflect on what's just happened.

 It'll be great! Just hang in there. The answers will be found in chaos!

What did you recognize?

○ **Earth** Elements are down-to-earth and practical. Answers and decisions are based on facts and results.

○ **Air** Elements help us to make sense of a situation with their logic and natural tendency to note risks and potential problems.

○ **Water** Elements are inclusive, calming and take time for reflection.

○ **Fire** Elements are forever hopeful and optimistic that all will turn out for the best.

At the Office

Rocky swaggered forward to see what the commotion was all about. Who were these people, anyway? He was focused on getting the job done and this noisy brawl outside his door angered him. Didn't they understand the project needed completing today? He stormed out to tell them to shut up!

Ariel was just doing a spell check on the document when a distraction outside caught his attention. Didn't they realize this was a place for work and concentration? How could he stay focused on the project with such disorder going on?! He decided to complete the calculation and then check on whether the outside chaos was warranted.

Brooke was head down, engrossed in the project. She knew if she did a good job, she'd get everyone's agreement on her part in the program. Brooke wondered if it was the team making all that noise out there. She liked the team, they were all so creative, but pretty volatile too. She hoped everybody would get back to work soon.

Blaze heard the laughter outside and curiosity got the best of her. Who were these people having so much fun...without her? Yes, yes, she needed to get this project under way but she was sure she had plenty of time. Sounded like a real show out there. A glance in the mirror, and she was out the door.

What did you recognize?

○ **Rocky** is a practical guy, and not afraid of raising his voice to get his way.

○ **Ariel** is busy using his brain and is not easily distracted when thinking.

○ **Brooke** always has an opinion about people. She likes to help but is shy.

○ **Blaze** likes to look good and seldom misses an opportunity for fun.

At the Restaurant with the Team

Rocky put aside the wine list and said, *We'll have the Premium Cab Sav. Oh, are you all happy with that? Fine.* He quickly scanned the menu and continued, *You all ready to order? I'll start with the venison and have the steak, well done.*

Ariel read the menu from right to left. This was a bit of a splurge for the team but they did decide that the social aspect of team was justified for the project's sake. That's fine…he'd order the lamb for which the restaurant won the Cuisine Award for Quality and Presentation. Hopefully the wine wouldn't be too bold for this dish.

Brooke studied the menu and was delighted the team decided to have a meal together. It's very bonding to socialize and interact in an informal setting. She really preferred white wine, but didn't want to make a fuss. The thought of Rocky eating Bambi was a bit depressing, but she knew the vegetarian special would be lovely… or maybe the fish.

Blaze was excited by the variety the menu offered. What was this they did with alligator meat? She hoped the waiter recognized her from her last visit and the generous tip she gave him. It would be impressive service, surely. *Can we have a basket of your great bread? Is everyone comfortable where they're sitting?*

What did you recognize?

○ **Rocky** is quick to make a decision and does not like to wait around for others to make up their minds. He is conservative but competitive and likes to be the best and have the best.

○ **Ariel** is always calculating the costs, the risks and benefits. Every decision is based on a fine appreciation for the quality and a clear understanding of the limitations.

○ **Brooke** strives for balance. Decision-making is a flexible process that eventually reaches a compatible conclusion.

○ **Blaze** is ever optimistic, and will always go for the latest and greatest, or something different.

Team Meeting

Can you recognize which Element is talking here?

🙂 *How about we have our next meeting over a meal and a few drinks! Let's each bring some new ideas about how to solve our problem and we'll discuss them then. I'm sure we'll come up with something*

🙂 *Can we have an agenda when we come to these meetings? I find that without one, we're always going off on tangents and never completing anything.*

🙂 *Shall I take the minutes? I can e-mail everyone a copy.*

🙂 *We'll go around once. Tell us what you've done since the last meeting and your next step.*

Who is talking?

○ Brainstorming is always a great way to generate new ideas for Fire. Especially over food and drinks!

○ Order, sequence and ticking off agenda items are important to Air. The group has a far better chance of covering everything required if focus is maintained and agenda points are clear.

○ Water is supportive, inclusive and wants to ensure that everyone is kept in the loop.

○ Succinct, to the point and direct, Earth is action-oriented and performance focused.

The Project Hiccup

☺ *I can see it now! If we make this slight change I'm suggesting, we'll just scoot around the problem and it opens up all sorts of opportunities!*

☺ *You've got to be joking. Look, I've already told you what we have to do. We can't afford to play around. Let's just get on with it.*

☺ *Calm down can't we discuss this a little further? Can we let everyone have a say before we make the final decision?*

☺ *Well in my judgement we need to wait until all the stats are in. Can't we just slow down, keep to the project plan and take the steps one at a time?*

Who is talking?

○ Recognize the optimism? A *slight* change. *Scoot around* the problem. But the last word is the give-away – Fire is into the possibilities, the *opportunities*.

○ *Get on with it* is an Earth trademark, and their strength is in telling people what to do. Where would we be without them?

○ Uncomfortable when the conversation heats up, Water asserts a calming influence and tries to be as inclusive as possible – *let everyone have a say*.

○ Analyzing information gives Air confidence. Speculation is an unnecessary risk, avoidable by keeping to the *plan*.

The Next Step

🙂 *How do you feel about the different options here? Have we considered all the alternatives?*

🙂 *I think we need to show some real pizzazz! Who is going to pay attention to us if we don't sharpen up our act and look good out there?*

🙂 *Hang on, what we have to do is watch the bottom line, work harder and stop wasting time on the warm fuzzies.*

🙂 *Why can't we just keep to the budget? Please stay on course. Do you think I spent those long hours budgeting and forecasting for nothing?*

Who's talking?

○ Water loves to include everyone and all different options.

○ Image is everything for Fire.

○ Earth never loses sight of the end result.

○ Systems are the defining point for Air.

The Trip

☺ *Think what others will say when they hear I'm going on this trip! I've always dreamed of dining with kings. 5 castles in 2 weeks! It's a bit pricey but what the heck.*

☺ *When do we get there? Just make sure we have a luxury car at the other end... and no bus trips.*

☺ *Oouu... it sounds a bit expensive but lovely. We'll have to make sure we stay within our price range. I'll write out all the options so we can discuss where we want to visit, what we want to see and how much it'll cost.*

☺ *Our airline points will allow us to go only so far. If we go at the same time as the special offer, we can take advantage of the coupons I have from last time. I'll get the travel insurance and photocopy the itinerary.*

Who is talking?

○ What the others say about them is very important to Fire. Who else would have such a wild imagination to dream about *dining with kings*?

○ Independence and control warrants a car... a bus trip with others does not fit in this equation.

○ Water is concerned that everyone can afford the trip and will enjoy it.

○ Economy and safety are high priorities for Air. They are meticulous enough to keep track of specials, coupons and where to get the best insurance.

Business Strategy

☺ *I've just taken the Business Plan to bits… there are too many loopholes and unrealistic expectations.*

☺ *How about a road show to share the vision? We can pull it together in no time.*

☺ *If our people are assets – why do we treat them as expenses? We're losing momentum here and it's because we haven't focused on our people*

☺ *Get the directors here tomorrow. Make sure they're prepared to lay out their strategic outcomes and action steps.*

Who's talking?

○ Air is an excellent investigator and examiner. Air's penchant for finding missing pieces and what won't work can prevent potential problems and delays.

○ If in doubt, take it on the road to inspire and gather the troops. Time is never an issue as there will always be a way for Fire.

○ Answers are usually found in discussion, consensus and valuing all those whom are involved. Water constantly reminds us of the real contributors – people.

○ The time is *now* for Earth. Be prepared with the facts, homework done and ready for action.

The Business

☺ *Look, unless you can give us better signals without the usual hemming and hawing, you won't be getting my boys producing anything.*

☺ *They don't have a clue about what it's costing us. When was the last time they read the budget report....and understood it? I'll send another memo.*

☺ *We've promised the earth and are giving them a few buckets of sand!! Come on people, you've seen our ads...where're the goods? What we've initiated is great but we want to create satisfied customers.*

☺ *It keeps coming back to our office. Why don't the departments talk to each other? Our support is being stretched beyond our limits.*

Who's talking?

○ In charge and controlling, Earth wants no surprises, just clear directives to ensure results and performance.

○ Clarifying situations for others usually comes easily in written form for Air. Reports, statistics, graphs and documentation spell things out in detail and should theoretically provide ample information from which to decide exactly what is needed.

○ Looking good is critical for Fire success. Feedback, be it individual or corporate, must be in the 'fantastic' range to keep the Fires burning brightly.

○ Saying no to anything is difficult for Water. Pleas for better communication are consistent though often too soft to be heard above the roar of miscommunication.

Managing

☺ *The flow charts and timeframes should be in by the end of the week in order to ensure we stay on time, on budget.*

☺ *I've heard from the other managers that the Board is questioning some of our decisions. We'd better regroup and re-charge the team.*

☺ *Let's have another meeting to discuss this issue. I want everyone's input before we make any decisions.*

☺ *How are the troops performing? Make sure the KPI's are set out and everyone's geared up to hit those targets.*

Who's talking?

○ Time is of the essence for Air. Sound management means keeping to schedules and plotting out the ups and downs of how systems are functioning.

○ Hints of something amiss makes Fire wonder if reputation is at stake. Re-inspiring colleagues to create visions of success is all-important for image.

○ Managing is about getting agreement and fostering commitment. Water manages through listening, consensus and valuing all contributions.

○ Life, business and success are all part of a competitive game… often a war game for Earth. Achievement and winning are the prizes.

Performance

😊 *Just give me my outcomes and I'll get there.*

😊 *I can do the job better if I'm reminded of the value I offer and am acknowledged every now and then for my contribution.*

😊 *Give me feedback. Lots of it. If I know what you want, I'll do my very best to give it to you. I'll help you to make this place shine!*

😊 *Unless I know why I'm asked to do something, it makes little sense for me to give it my best. Give me time and give me reasons.*

Who's talking?

○ Confidence, resourcefulness and sheer perseverance gets Earth to desired outcomes. Performance is about getting things done, using whoever or whatever is needed to succeed.

○ Valuing the contributions of Water will keep the river flowing. Hard work and loyalty are the outcomes if communication dams give way to openness and honesty.

○ Feedback with room for creativity is a catalyst for Fire. Routine, repetition of effort will fizzle the flames, whereas opportunities for creative solutions can ignite. Be ready for ingenious solutions… but ensure smoke alarms are set.

○ Answer all *why* questions for Air. Once understood, focus and consistency will achieve the required outcomes.

Earth Air Water Fire

Customer Service

🙂 *Hi Miss Hamilton! This is Jackie from Glitz Styles. Because you're one of our favored customers, we're just letting you know about our special sale next week....*

🙂 *That particular model has all the functions you want and is the best in its class. I can have it delivered tomorrow afternoon.*

🙂 *The service warranty will cover all parts for 3 years. Here's a brochure with all the specifications. Take your time, I'll be right here if you have any questions.*

🙂 *Our service person's name is George. If you have any problems, which I doubt you will, here's his phone number. You can call him anytime – even if only to ask him a question.*

Who's the customer?

○ Feeling special, on a first name basis is a key for Fire's assessment of service excellence. Helping Fire to look good will maintain that impressive, squinting brightness that Fire loves!

○ Functionality, status and service back-up will do for Earth.

○ Guarantees and proof of quality help Air to assess future service requirements. Good service is efficient, accurate and timely.

○ Personal assurances of service follow-up are important to Water. Continued support shows that customer care is a part of a value-based culture.

Sales

☺ *Have a seat. Now, you say you've shopped around and compared. What do you like about the product so far and what will you be looking for in the product long-term?*

☺ *It's the latest model, just came in this week! It surpasses the previous models with these amazing new features that'll save you time. What do you think of the new colors and style?!*

☺ *What specifically will you be using this for? When you compare this brand to that, the quality of this one is clearly higher in standard. Let me show you the user manual to explain why...*

☺ *This one does exactly what you want and I can have it delivered this afternoon. Cash or credit?*

Who's the customer?

○ *I care and want to be cared for* says Water. Never quite sure if the right decision has been made, Water likes a friendly chat to build confidence. Earth and Fire are less patient.

○ This Fire sales style focuses on the latest, greatest, new improved product. Great rapport with Fire, but Air would find the approach flighty and the product unproven.

○ Very clear, very specific. An Air approach for an Air customer. Remembering that a Fire would probably lose the manual in a week, this approach would not excite.

○ Earth. This is fast, no frills sales. Probably too fast for Water or Air... for different reasons.

Leadership

☺ *Well done is better than well said.*

☺ *I have a dream!*

☺ *There go my people. I must follow them for I am their leader.*

☺ *He who controls others may be powerful, but he who has mastered himself is mightier still.*

Who's talking?

○ Benjamin Franklin. Results say more than the build up. Earth.

○ Martin Luther King Jr. A leader who inspires others to follow the quest. Fire.

○ Mahatma Ghandi. Leading from behind with strong conviction is powerful. Water.

○ Lao Tsu. Understand first. Air.

The Personal Growth Seminar

☺ *I know exactly who I am and where I'm going thank you. If it'll grow sales though, I'll give it go.*

☺ *This visualization stuff is great! I usually get so energized and inspired!*

☺ *I know I sometimes get emotional at these things, but I feel it'll help my confidence levels.*

☺ *Where's all this information from? Is this a cult?*

Who's talking?

○   If the result is attractive, Earth is willing.

○   Inspiring and being inspired is so Fire – anything to stimulate the imagination.

○   Being so sensitive, self-confidence is a challenge for Water.

○   Rely on Air for skepticism to keep us honest.

The Restructure

☺ *I think some of the changes are necessary, but people are hurting and there's no safety net for them. I'm not sure we're doing the right thing.*

☺ *Well... don't we only need people who really love their jobs? This cake's delicious!*

☺ *All this stop, start, change, stop, start, gets us nowhere. Anyway, the contracts spell it out in black & white. Why can't we stick to them?*

☺ *Results so far are dismal. Face the facts, we have to make changes* **now.** *Performance has to improve -* **this month.**

Who's talking?

○ Being unsure and worrying about people hurting is typically Water.

○ Enthusiasm for the job is a given for Fire. Distractions are conveniently found everywhere.

○ Air likes to be orderly. Randomly stopping and starting again is very irritating and variations are unnecessary if flexibility is built into the plan.

○ Direct and to the point, Earth hones in on the demonstrable reality and the immediate needs, without flinching.

Moving the Office

☺ *I need a quiet corner to think. And there has to be space for my books and filing cabinet.*

☺ *Make sure my phone is connected. The open plan looks great! Where's the coffee machine?*

☺ *I'm happy sharing space as long as the others are quiet and considerate.*

☺ *Give me a big desk in my own room.*

Who's talking?

○ Clear space for clear thinking is what Air needs.

○ Fire likes an audience and stimulus to keep going.

○ Peaceful harmony is what Water seeks.

○ Earth is practical and knows the value of status.

Maintaining Self-Balance

☺ *I'm not sure. Let's look at the process again rather than decide immediately.*
Later: All right, I'll put a stake in the ground to show what I stand for.

☺ *This is taking too long; I'll just do it myself and finish it now.*
Later: I'm sorry I didn't allow you to finish the task but I needed it done quickly. Can you tell me how you feel about the outcome and how we might have gotten a faster result?

☺ *The rules are written here. It can't be any clearer.*
Later: Perhaps if we look at this from a different perspective, we can stay within the rules but find a way to keep the process rolling.

☺ *Hey! I've got a great idea! Let's try something completely different instead of the same old, same old.*
Later: Actually, experience proves that it is a good solution… it just needs a little modification to leverage even better results!

Who's talking?

○ Putting off a decision is one way of allowing time for further input. Water wants to ensure decision making involves everyone, but at some point in time, a stake must be put in the ground to keep moving toward the desired outcomes.

○ Impatience and the need to complete often motivates Earth to take things in hand and make it work. Taking time to include and benefit from the skills of others may find better solutions in the long run.

○ Rules and systems are definitely needed to keep things on track, however if these begin to thwart success, it might be wise to explore new avenues of thought and action. Like a cool breeze, Air can refresh the situation by relaxing into new frames of thought.

○ As a catalyst to new ideas, Fire ignites energy. Focussing that energy and staying on the agreed path is often ample motivation to keep things moving forward.

Fun

☺ *Janice enjoyed the quiet of it all. She found the serenity and beauty of her artwork an ideal way to spend leisure time.*

☺ *Max let out a holler, fist of victory in the air, as he watched his team score another goal. He slapped his neighbor's back as an* I told you they'd do it! *reminder. Cracking another joke about the inadequacies of the opposing team, Max sat back with a wide grin of satisfaction on his face.*

☺ *Jodie tightened her calf muscles once more to the beat of Robbie Williams blaring through the speakers. She kept to the rhythm, it hurt but it felt good. The energy in the room was electric and the instructor looked good. What a buzz... and afterwards, the best cappuccino in town!*

☺ *Carl loved watching his family play. It was an important time for them all... to have fun together and enjoy each other. Preparing for the outing was half the fun because he knew those little touches of care would ensure a great day for all.*

Who's talking?

○ Fun is often reflected in the form of individual or small group enjoyment for Air. Quality and skill are appreciated and can provide hours of entertainment.

○ Pushing and pointing outward reflects fun that is daring. Earth likes competition. Earth likes to win.

○ Looking good, exerting energy, and being with others are usually important to a Fire's sense of fun and happiness.

○ Spending time with people or pets one loves is a soothing form of fun for Water. Joy is found in camaraderie, shared stories and general concern for creating harmony and fun.

Humor

☺ *Come on! Grab a hat and let's pretend! You be the serious one, I'll play the fool.*

☺ *Why did the chicken cross the road?*

☺ *Did you hear the one about the fellow who shot himself in the foot?…*

☺ *Yes, in a previous life I was that person you're speaking of…*

Who's talking?

○ Playing the clown comes easily for Fire. Anything to maintain an environment of laughter and fun.

○ Storytelling and humor often go hand in hand for Water. Punch lines are hard to remember in the telling, but Water Elements make wonderful audiences.

○ Pushing and pointing out inadequacies or misfortunes often comes through in Earth humor. A hearty laugh either at themselves or at the expense of others is not a problem.

○ Air can excel in witty puns, satire and tongue in cheek humor.

Money

☺ *I'm looking for a low risk, long term investment. My concerns are security and ensuring the money is there when I need it.*

☺ *Do your homework. Diversify, weigh the risks, then buy.*

☺ *I want to make sure my family has money available for a rainy day. I can put aside a little each month and put it into some long term, safe bonds.*

☺ *We deserve it! Let's put this trip on the credit card and recharge our batteries.*

Who's talking?

○ There is usually great clarity about how money is allotted, saved and earned for Air. Steps to ensure wise spending and risk management are a part of Air's financial planning.

○ Money is a means by which to achieve desired outcomes or the reward itself. Earth knows how to spend, where and for what.

○ The more conservative nature of water in terms of money ensures that it is kept for needed or special occasions. Often, family and close friends come first for hard-earned savings.

○ Generous with money if it impresses, makes a difference or creates happiness, Fire can't help but look to the bright side of spending!

Fear

☺ *Get a hold of yourself. Focus on how we'll deal with this and stop mumbling about regrets.*

☺ *Everything is going wrong. I've checked the list. Most of the initiatives are either incomplete or have failed. We're doomed.*

☺ *What problem? It'll be fine! Don't worry! Let's go out and think about it later with fresh minds.*

☺ *I feel so tired… like I'm being pulled down into a whirlpool. I'm afraid of what might happen if things keep going on like this.*

Who's talking?

○ Staying in control, even in a state of fear, is important for Earth. Regaining momentum and focus on outcomes helps to work through problems.

○ Beginning by eliminating the wrongs first is often a tactic used by Air. Though perceived as being negative, Air finds this approach a way of honing down for substance.

○ Easily distracted and dodging hard decision making, Fire uses optimism to find another time to deal with fear, or ignore it all together. Fire can rationalize and create enough smoke to feel the fear and do it anyway.

○ In search of meaning and answers, hours of thought and discussion often surround Water when succumbed by fear.

Trust

🙂 *I hope you trust that we're all doing our best on this. It's really going to be a team effort and I'll certainly do my part to support the process. The best we can do is to keep our communication open and honest. I'm sure everything will turn out for the best if we work together.*

🙂 *It's a gut feel, but I'm confident it's right. I need to be in control... when that control is taken away or threatened, it's like a red rag to a bull. Trust me... let me do it my way. The results will be there for you.*

🙂 *I trust that I can do the job to your standards. The rules are very clear to me and I'm sure we can comply so that the final result is exactly what we want. If we all do our own bit, I guarantee the quality and result will be well worth the effort.*

🙂 *No need to worry. I have a good feeling about this and believe it's worth the energy we're putting in. You're doing such a great job, we all are. I trust you to keep up the energy and that we'll get it right. I'm optimistic that we'll reach our vision and really make a difference out there!*

Who's talking?

○ Trust is mutual and is strongest when established and developed as a value. For Water, trust is like fine crystal... beautiful and strong, but if broken, very difficult to repair.

○ Trust is strong and assumed because bold Earth clearly states expectations from the beginning. Trust is gained from achievement and deeds.

○ Ask questions first, measure trust later. For Air, trust is built with adherence to rules, follow-through on guarantees, and solutions that are on time, on budget.

○ Trust first, ask questions later. Fire inherently trusts that, like them, everyone is as enthusiastic and committed as they are. Bubbles of enthusiasm may burst when trust is broken, but Fire's optimism will find a way to find more soapy water... and create more bubbles.

Who's Spoken?

Are all those snippets of conversation fact, fiction or fantasy?   They are a combination of all three, however they do reflect the state of communication in many homes and workplaces.

Fiction and fantasy abound in communication, even as people look each other straight in the eye and create worlds mildly or wildly discordant with others. Perhaps it would be easier to just sit back and enjoy conversations for what they are worth in helping us understand people. Detachment, combined with an understanding of the Elements often helps to avoid or remove hooks that pull at our emotional strings.

There are also forms of communication that are violent and scarring. Communication violence is what spurs us to continue our work with the TetraMap of Nature. We often observe in disbelief, the inhumanity reflected in the world and wonder how it's come to be and where it will take us. The four Elements, Earth, Air, Water and Fire give us pause... Nature in its glory, works synergistically to create breathtaking beauty. When Nature becomes a metaphor for behavior and systems, it seems easier to understand diversity in a positive light and work towards creating parallel synergy in how we live together.

Earth, Air, Water, Fire have helped us to make some sense of the insanity of world conditions by encouraging us to first look to ourselves, our communications and the results we have created. Along our personal journeys, it's been a reward in itself to watch clients grasp TetraMap concepts and embrace the learning that comes from working with the model. Many have strengthened their teams, their organizations, their families, and most importantly, themselves.

We all have, at some stage, behaved in ways that reflect each of the four Elements – Earth, Air, Water and Fire. Some of our behavior we're proud of, some not. The presentation of various life scenarios and continued development of the TetraMap is our attempt to support better communication. "Better", meaning communication that is humane, compassionate and that adds value.

When Earth, Air, Water and Fire clash in earthquakes, tornadoes, floods and volcanic eruptions, we have different forms of violence and destruction. Those imbalances too are natural but as thinking beings, we bounce back seeking new ways to predict and prepare. The TetraMap of Nature is a tool to also help us predict and prepare for positive communication and life outcomes.

Celebrate the strengths that are inherent in Earth, Air, Water and Fire and strive to synergize the life force that surrounds each one. Build upon what you've learned so far from the Elements by practicing their 5 tips for happiness:

1. Earth: Be strong, happy, confident in your Element.
2. Air: Understand each Element to improve the quality of your life.
3. Water: Be compassionate with yourself and others.
4. Fire: Like Nature, synergize the Elements to create value.
   and
5. Look within to the Nature of your life. You'll find answers, balance and your own special uniqueness.

© 2004 TetraMap Int'l

Approaching the Elements

Now that you have the gist of the elements of human nature, you can probably recognize some obvious Earth, Air, Water and Fire characteristics. The question is, now what?

First, let's consider some of our common personal triggers to each Element. Often, when we meet someone of the same or similar Element, rapport is built pretty quickly. Vibes are good, conversation flow is smooth and easy. However, what about when we meet face to face with a direct, almost shouting Earth Element, or a pensive, non-responding Air Element, or a quiet, shy Water Element, or an all-over-the-place, fast-talking Fire Element?

Of course, how one reacts depends on the person, the history, the baggage, one's mood and a multitude of other factors. Reactions to other Elements might range from sheer delight, to eyes rolling up to incredible heights toward one's eyebrows. Whatever the triggered reactions might have been to date, you are now in a much better position to *respond* to each Element…correct? You now know that each Element has natural preferences, motivations and needs, and you ARE wiser for this information. Let's begin now to celebrate diversity and the strength that every person brings to a situation.

We'll look at each Element and list some specific strategies that might help you to build rapport quickly.

Approaching Earth

Approaching EARTH: Be...
- ○ direct
- ○ prepared
- ○ confident
- ○ to the point

It might be an idea not to be...
- ○ inaudible
- ○ unprepared
- ○ touchy-feely
- ○ rambling

Questions are important in enrolling anyone into a conversation. Here are some questions that might help you to guide an Earth Element to a positive outcome:
- ○ What specifically are the results you're aiming for?
- ○ If you were in control of situation (or, as you're in control of the situation) what do you think is the best strategy to get the outcome we want?
- ○ This may be a bit more risky, but what do you think about...
- ○ It's a big challenge. How can we face this head on together?
- ○ What do you think this solution would look like from the receiving end?

A meeting comes to mind where I was briefed by a Water/Fire Element. Her goal was to organize a team/personal development workshop for the senior management of a corporation. Not surprisingly, Human Resources management was her forte. Though her research gave evidence that such a workshop would be a turning point in the corporation's culture development, this manager sought counsel from the Earth/Fire Sales Director.

I didn't really understand why there was such concern and was surprised to see both these managers accompany me to the meeting with the CEO whom I'd never before met. When I walked in the door, I realized immediately why they'd come to my side, though still not sure if it was to protect themselves or me.

The CEO was huge. He walked over slowly, sat and looked directly at me. I assumed I was to speak first after a very short, fast introduction by the Sales Director. I thought, *Earth is firm, decisive, results oriented. Just get to the point.* I looked directly at this mountain of a man, told him what I could do, the results he would get and how long it would take. I asked him 2 questions relating to his and the company's desired outcomes. The conversation took approximately 10 minutes.

He mentioned he'd checked my references, then he got up, and walked away. I thought it was over. My tactic hadn't worked. I was ready to leave. He reached across his desk, picked up his diary, turned to me and said, *Dates.*

The three of us walked out, the other two with huge grins. Staff were outside the door. They got a positive nod from the managers and I heard gasps and saw looks of surprise all around. I congratulated the 'Earth within' and went on to work with this firm for several years.

Approaching Air

Approaching AIR: Be...
- focused
- timely
- succinct
- sequential

It might be an idea not to...
- demand immediate action
- exaggerate
- over-generalize
- change subjects quickly

Questions that may help guide the conversation to a positive outcome:
- What do you think about this?
- How would you modify the plans to better accommodate this situation?
- How much more time would you need to...
- Can you explain the logic behind this?
- What was the big picture outcome for this?

Air Elements respond well to evenly paced, prepared, well-constructed trains of thought and logic. Stick to the point and stay focused on the subject. This may be quite a challenge for those who naturally and easily jump from one thought to another in the same breath. When speaking to an Air Element, it would be helpful to stay on track by starting and ending a sentence speaking about the same subject.

Imagine a meeting at which an Air Element, in true Air fashion reminds the others that the rules and policies forbid the action they are discussing. The Fire Element, exasperated with eyes rolling up, starts to pace and explain that rules are meant to be broken. The Earth Element reiterates that they'll do whatever it takes to get the results - rules or no rules. The Water Element fetches the rules and policy documents.

The Air Element is of course, 100% correct. But perhaps if the policies were adhered to, the entire project would come to a stand still. Enrolling Air to think outside the policies takes time and a strategy, and good group questioning.

Recognize and acknowledge the need for structure and rules, but reaffirm the big picture and overall strategy. Because timeframes are important to Air, discuss what would need to happen in order to reach objectives and stay within the set timeframe. This may mean a totally different approach to the issue and include a way of bypassing the rule that is thwarting the process. An Air Element may have just the focus, perseverance, intelligence and attention to detail required to find even the smallest of loopholes to avoid the obstacle.

Approaching Water

Approaching WATER: Be...
- sensitive to feelings
- kind
- inclusive
- attentive

It might be an idea not to be...
- too bold and loud
- demanding
- discourteous
- in a rush

Questions to help the conversation stay on track:
- So how are you feeling about... (specific incident or idea)?
- What was our original goal?
- What are the key points that encapsulate what we just discussed?
- What if we *could* do what you thought was too difficult? What would be the first step in getting there?
- In the big picture of things, do you believe that's the best course to take?

How to approach a Water Element? Be open, interested, and LISTEN! Steer away from conflict and consider what might be perceived to be fair and equitable. Walk softly but NOT with a big stick. Give plenty of time for thought and process.

Water flows on and on and so can conversations with Water Elements. If its solutions you're looking for, gently steer the conversation back to the original objectives. It would help to start the dialog with an overview of the desired outcomes of the conversation.

Take opportunities to give recognition for good work or ideas and acknowledgment of the value that Water brings to the table. I once observed a scenario that reflected this approach in a planning session… it was beautiful. Though the more outspoken people were Earth and Fire, this group of leaders were enlightened enough to respect everyone in the room.

The focus of the meeting naturally revolved around strategies, tactics, timeframes and planning. When discussion came to dissemination of information, two Water Element managers showed extreme concern about the people side of the business. They obviously did not want to rock the boat, however, as leaders they took a stance and showed considerable emotion as they explained what they saw to be flaws in the cultural integrity of the organization.

In the past, this same leadership group would have given appropriate 'lip-service' to subjects of team, culture and values, but in an enlightened moment, the penny seemed to drop… it was Eureka! time.

The Water Elements were approached with respect and acknowledgment for the work they'd done to keep the corporate machine running smoothly. Their concern and care for people was evident and appreciated. The group asked several questions regarding the integration of the strategies in light of the overall corporate vision.

There was, if you will, a blending of the Elements. By the end of the meeting the strategies encompassed all the Elements and inspired action-taking and people enrolment.

Water is inclusive and flowing. Patience, leadership and appreciation of an interdependent culture can open enormous floodgates of Water energy and commitment.

Approaching Fire

Approaching FIRE: Be…

- adventurous
- optimistic
- trusting
- animated

It might be an idea not to be…

- closed to ideas
- monotonous
- negative
- considering an overhead transparency presentation

Questions that will help to keep things on track:

- What would be the first 3 steps to getting there?
- What's most fun about this job/project/idea?
- How will this help us to reach our vision?
- What was the first issue at hand?
- Can you start at the beginning and give me the sequence of events?

Fire Elements are very easily distracted, thus when approaching Fire, make sure you're not offended by wandering eyes, movements, walking about the room or quick changes of subject. Approach with a positive attitude, smiles and trusting that this dialog will have a happy ending.

Ideas will abound, so be prepared to maintain your own sense of order and sequence. Ask for a slower rendition if necessary, or ask the Fire to write or draw their concepts to help slow the process down. Make your own sentences short, and succinct to help keep things on track.

Fire loves feedback - the more positive the better, though constructive criticism is much appreciated. Let ideas fly that will remedy situations and discuss opportunities to demonstrate understanding. Inject a sense of fun where appropriate to keep things alive and moving.

A quick story comes to mind. Two people talking, one trying to convince a Fire Element to do something pretty mundane and unexciting. Lots of questions and ideas were offered, like - *What if… How about changing the way… Did you know that* (so and so; famous person) *once did the same thing? After we finish, let's celebrate!* and *In the big picture of things, this will really make a difference…*

When approaching a Fire Element, maintain a brightness of future. Give hope with bright energy!

Flexibility

Of course no one style of approach will usually make it. That's because:

○ We all have aspects of all four Elements… in different degrees.

○ Our second preferred style might make all the difference to a situation depending on the subject, the stress levels, and the current state of the individual.

For instance, a Fire/Water Element may respond to a situation with more care and concern than a Fire/Earth Element who may just *go for it!*

Therefore understanding how one might approach each of the Elements is just the first step to better communication. A more important step is to practice flexibility in approaching and listening to all the Elements.

Flexibility is a major key to successful relationship building. Understanding the strengths of Earth, Air, Water, Fire is a start to your flexibility. Putting aside any tendency to blame others for their behaviors or responses is also a good beginning. Consideration of the following may help you to do this.

Think of the last time someone significantly pushed your anger or hurt buttons. Who was it? How did you react? Maybe you can't even remember the reason, but you definitely reacted in a way that was physically or emotionally memorable to you. You felt your face get red, your heart started to pound so loudly that you could hear it, you cried or were so taken aback, you froze, unable to speak.

Did you verbally lash out, yell, walk away, think terrible thoughts about this person? Maybe or maybe not, the thing is, was there ANYTHING there to indicate that this person was exhibiting certain Elemental traits? Perhaps the Earth Element said something very coldly, bluntly to get what was needed. Or was it an Air Element making a judgement statement to crystallize what the problem was? Maybe a Water Element couldn't make a decision because there were too many variables to consider or a completely off-the-wall Fire Element babbling about another crazy idea.

All in all, what are the chances that this person was actually demonstrating an attribute or preference that was, in fact, a strength of that Element? For instance:

 The Earth Element was blunt and seemingly uncaring because there was an outcome or result at stake. Remembering that Earth Elements are very results-oriented and focused, anything that may get in the way of achieving is at risk of being pushed aside.

 The Air Element may need more detail, make judgements and seem incredibly critical, but remember that the focus of attention is in detail and staying on path with tried and true methods. Emotion is not usually a factor nor important in their strategy.

 The Water Element wants always to remain constant and inclusive. When pushed into a corner to make decisions, all the attributes that support agreement, consensus, what's best for the greatest number may take time.

 The Fire Element, searching for new solutions, new ways, breaking boundaries, is constantly catalyzing new ideas…often just by thinking aloud.

Each of these Elements may be just living out their natural preferences, almost to the point they really can't help themselves. It's their strength! … though perhaps inappropriately timed or placed.

Are we flexible enough to accept their style with elegance and grace, or are we so entrenched in our usual reactions, that it's impossible to budge. If it's a practiced entrenchment, flexibility doesn't come easily. 'Practiced' meaning that we've mastered a set response, be it anger, tears, inability to speak, so many times that we're excellent at it. We're so practiced in fact, that it may only take one word, or just a look to trigger us into our practiced response.

Michael Durst's book, *Napkin Notes: On the Art of Living* has an excellent description and explanation of triggered responses. We go unconscious and slip right into our practiced response. Michael states that only after we regain consciousness, can we ask ourselves, *What was happening just before I went unconscious?*

What Elemental triggers make you go unconscious?

Earth: Bluntness, raised voice, pointing finger, wants action or decision now!

Air: Critical, asking why, attention to detail, wants more proof and time.

Water: Hesitant, emotional, long explanations, warm-fuzzy sensitivity.

Fire: Easily distracted, scattered, dreaming, no sense of time, attention seeking.

Flexibility is understanding that the above traits are part of the natural strengths of these Elements. Each of those preferences can also save our lives when in situations that warrant bluntness, attention to detail, emotion or dreaming up new ideas. Understanding the Elements coupled with your skill to respond, rather than react, is the epitome of flexibility and can save you from stress and unease.

Without flexibility, your anger and upset may, in fact, lead to more than unease, but to dis-ease. When we allow ourselves to get so upset that our physicality changes, heats up, stiffens, strikes out, increases heartrate... we might as well rip out our adrenals and offer them to the offending trigger. While you're at it, you may as well give the trigger your thymus and all other glands that are a part of your immune system, because that is what you are virtually doing anyway.

Flexibility is understanding the Earth, Air, Water and Fire within you and in those around you. It is gracefully recognizing the strength behind actions and words and moving with confidence to a space where you respond to match that Elemental need. Meet Earth with Earth firmness and focus, meet Air with logic and questions, meet Water with caring and feelings, meet Fire with hope and possibilities.

When You Listen to Others

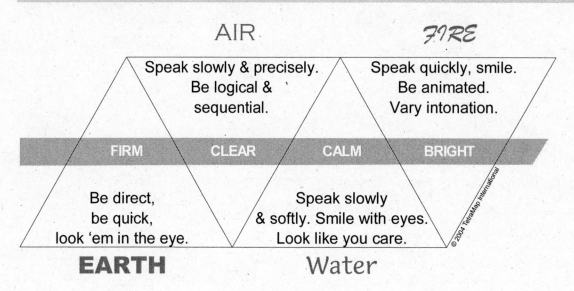

AIR — Speak slowly & precisely. Be logical & sequential.

FIRE — Speak quickly, smile. Be animated. Vary intonation.

FIRM | CLEAR | CALM | BRIGHT

EARTH — Be direct, be quick, look 'em in the eye.

Water — Speak slowly & softly. Smile with eyes. Look like you care.

© 2004 TetraMap International

When You Speak to Others

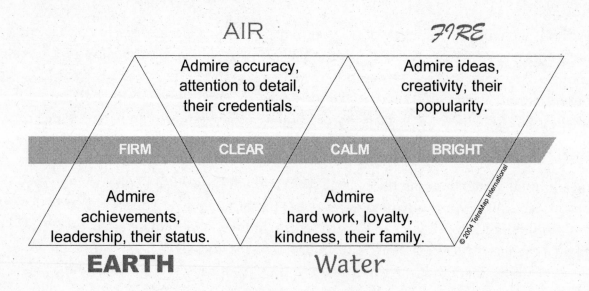

AIR — Admire accuracy, attention to detail, their credentials.

FIRE — Admire ideas, creativity, their popularity.

FIRM | CLEAR | CALM | BRIGHT

EARTH — Admire achievements, leadership, their status.

Water — Admire hard work, loyalty, kindness, their family.

© 2004 TetraMap International

When You Correct Others

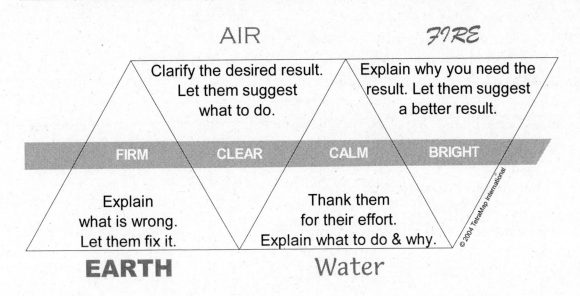

When You Motivate Others

The Elements of Teamwork

The focus so far has been on individual behavioral preferences reflected in the metaphor of Nature's Elements, Earth, Air, Water and Fire. The TetraMap of Teamwork focuses on the behavioral preferences of a team. A team that consists primarily of Earth and Air individuals may be very goal and bottom-line focused. This team may even be perceived as one that spends time on planning and executing those plans... no matter what obstacles may get in the way. In contrast, another team consisting primarily of Fire and Water individuals, may be perceived as great at discussing the big picture with any and all who care. Their interests may be more customer and service focused.

The balance of course, is found when any one team can share and blend the strengths all four Elements. The TetraMap of Teamwork supports groups to blend the natural preferences of the individuals so that the team can more effectively work together.

Let's step out of individual behavioral preferences and use the TetraMap of Team to help us map out how a team can reflect the synergy of Nature. This TetraMap helps us to define what specifically a team can do to create a balanced strategy for success. How a team aligns its goals, rules, values and spirit can make all the difference to its productivity and sustainability.

Creating productive, high-performance teams is a process and like most things in life, takes time and energy. Whether a team is handpicked for excellence or thrown together due to particular circumstances, there are ways, means, and maps to help.

High-performing teams have an innate or learned understanding of the four Elements from both an individual perspective and a team perspective. A team uses its members' strengths to its advantage. In parallel, the team plants seeds for synergy with its Earth/Air goals, directions, rules and reasoning, and its Water/Fire values, unity, spirit and motivation.

TetraMap® of Team

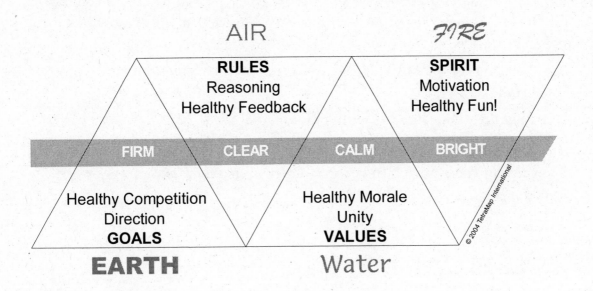

ogether the

lements

chieve

ore

In a high performance team, the diversity of Elemental attributes defines the team culture and creates the potential for team synergy.

Each individual in a team has a unique combination of strengths and each team as a group has a unique combination of strengths. Looking at a team as an entity, where are its greatest strengths? The team must have:

○ Firm goals and direction, and healthy competition.

○ Clear rules and reasoning, and healthy feedback.

○ Calm values and unity, and healthy morale.

○ Bright spirit and motivation, and healthy fun.

Earth: **FIRM GOALS**

Members of a high performance team are strongly committed to a set of common goals, both long and short term. A team goal needs to be firm like a mountain that beckons to be climbed. It must be:

○ **Challenging** If it is not challenging enough, another mountain may distract the team.

○ **Defined** Let's not climb the wrong mountain by mistake.

○ **Agreed** Preferably unanimously and enthusiastically.

○ **Rewarding** There must be a perceived benefit in either the process or outcome or both.

 Air: **CLEAR RULES**

Members of a high performance team clearly understand the rules, both written and unwritten. A team rule must be clear like the wind.

○ **Steady Direction** The intended outcome must be unambiguous.

○ **Transparent** It is clear where it is coming from, why it is important.

○ **Flows around obstacles** Still applies in difficult situations.

○ **Refreshes** Improves the situation and creates new opportunities.

 Water: **CALM VALUES**

Members of a high performance team are calmly committed to shared values. A team value must be calm like the ocean.

○ **Commands Respect** Not easily ignored.

○ **Pure** Doesn't have unwanted side effects.

○ **Deep** More than surface pretence.

○ **Reflects** Illuminates what is important.

▼ Fire: **BRIGHT SPIRIT**

A high performance team is renowned for its bright spirit. Team spirit must be bright like a campfire.

- ○ **Warming** Provides energy but requires effort to keep it bright.
- ○ **Enlightening** Sheds light on experiences and why they are important.
- ○ **Magnetic** Draws the team together toward a common purpose.
- ○ **A Beacon** Attracts attention from afar.

Listening in on a Team Meeting

Notice how each Element contributes to the team. Recognize who's talking?

☺ *How about we have our next meeting over a meal and a few drinks! Let's each bring some new ideas about how to solve our problem and we'll discuss them then. I'm sure we'll come up with something.*

☺ *Can we have an agenda when we come to these meetings? I find that without one, we're always going off on tangents and never completing anything.*

☺ *Shall I take the minutes? I can e-mail everyone a copy afterwards.*

☺ *We'll go around once. Tell us what you've done since the last meeting and your next step.*

Who's talking?

- ○ SPIRIT Fire ignites the motivation to keep going with fun and inspiration.
- ○ RULES Air plans and makes sure the team is prepared for every possible scenario.
- ○ CULTURE Water is always there for you, loyal and quietly but effectively keeps the team together.
- ○ GOALS Earth is decisive and emphatic on what action needs to be taken.

Building Team Synergy

 Earth: **FIRM GOALS**

Goal and direction setting give teams momentum and sustain effort. There must be a sense of stretch and challenge, but set within the achievable. Strategic planning is a process that firms up structure and foundations, enabling a team to be ready, aim and fire. Goals described in the team's plan should make the way forward exciting, worthwhile and hold the team together with a *can do* attitude. Be specific and clear about targets, milestones, responsibilities and accountabilities.

To create synergy: Blend the goals of Earth with the planning skills of Air, the commitment of Water and the lure of Fire.

 Air: **CLEAR RULES**

Unwritten rules can be as powerful as those written in black and white. Create rules together. Be comprehensive by including HOW these rules will be demonstrated. Write 5-10 rules together, ensuring definitions are clear and shared. Include how flexibility will play its part in living and assessing the rules.

To create synergy: Follow the rules with the structure of Earth, the patience of Water, and the lateral thinking of Fire so that rules do not inhibit but promote innovation and growth.

 Water: **CALM VALUES**

Have conversations about and announce team values. Never assume. More importantly, clarify definition of a few key values rather a long list of nice, want-to-be words. What *integrity* or *open and honest communication* means to one team member may be at total odds with another member. Model and demonstrate how each person, and the team, will be congruent with the values.

To create synergy: Integrate team values with the goals from Earth, reminders of agreements from Air, and encouragement from Fire that the values will keep the team on path toward its Vision.

 Fire: **BRIGHT SPIRIT**

Look at the glow of any winning team. That glow reflects the spirit of the team. Maintaining bright spirit takes lots of energy and lots and lots of trust. A compelling vision, created together will help to maintain the spirit. All the Elemental perspectives listed above will build trust.

To create synergy: Catalyze bright spirit by getting firm direction from Earth, reasonable and clear rules from Air, and by modeling congruency with team values from Water.

Earth Air Water Fire

Visionary Team Planning Process

Chapter Overview

○ Cooperative Creativity

○ What Does the Future Look Like?

○ How are we going to Get There?

○ Empowering Leaders & Followers

Setting a goal is one of the first steps toward creating the future. Creating an organization's plan for the future is much like an artist painting a picture. Usually there are some initial ideas about both the end result and the intended process.

○ Perhaps the intention is to recreate a photograph in a particular artistic style.

○ Perhaps the intention is to simply stand at the easel with brush and oils ready and give the imagination free reign, letting the picture evolve, stroke by stroke.

Whichever approach an organization chooses, the quality of the end result is usually dependent on a **common** intention and a **coordinated** implementation. The TetraMap of Visionary Team Planning suggests how to orchestrate a process for creating a common intention (shared vision) and a coordinated implementation (strategic plan). It is best done with a team of 12-24 people, although any size can work.

The TetraMap of Visionary Team Planning

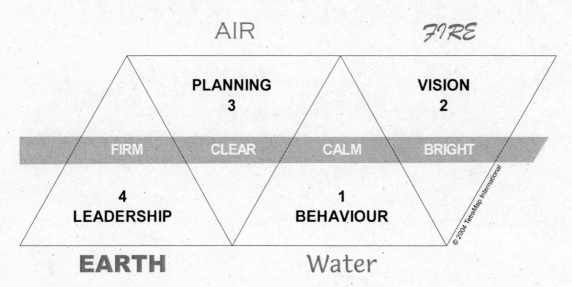

 Water: **BEHAVIOR**

When a group of people plan the future of an organization, each individual makes a personal investment in that future and is in fact, leading the way. Encouraging participation in planning the future is one way to promote leadership and responsible behavior.

Cooperative Creativity (see page 110) To begin, the team is divided into four Element groups, depending on each person's primary Elemental preferences.

 Fire: **VISION**

The future is first created in the imagination. We all have our own point of view, so why not combine different perspectives of the future for added depth and meaning?

What Does the Future Look Like? (see page 112) Each Element group creates their Element of the team vision and presents it for everyone to discuss.

Air: **PLANNING**

Now that we have a clear picture of where we are heading, how are we going to get there? A balanced strategy has a better chance of considering all the significant influences along the way.

How are we going to Get There? (see page 115) People then change into mixed groups to create strategies and action steps for implementing each Element of the team vision.

Earth: **LEADERSHIP** Taking responsibility for making it happen requires empowering leaders and followers.

Empowering Leaders & Followers (see page 119) Each person declares their personal commitment to leading toward the vision.

Cooperative Creativity

Everybody has a point of view. Cooperatively creating a picture of the future captures the inherent synergy between diverse points of view. What if the views are opposing? This is often what people are afraid of, but there are always aspects that complement each other. This complementary overlay of views inevitably adds new dimensions and magnifies meaning. By capitalizing on natural strengths and preferences, we can then collaborate to create a far more practical and compelling vision for the future.

Divide the team into four Element groups with similar viewpoints. For example, use the instrument in the *Why Are You Like That?* Workbooks or the on-line learning course at www.tetramap.com. Any four-type behavioral model will work if the types can be translated to the TetraMap's Earth, Air, Water, Fire terminology.

The TetraMap® of Behavior

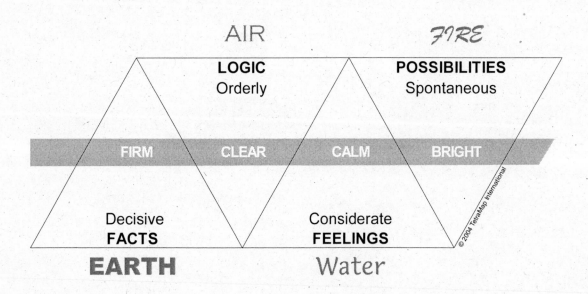

Natural View Points

Although you may be looking at a shared future, each person is coming from a different place and has a unique point of view.

 Earth: **FIRM FACTS**

Where is a mountain to climb? Show me the money! Earths set their sights on tangible achievements. They like to push out towards a firm goal, preferably the biggest and the best. The process is whatever they decide is practical at the time.

 Air: **CLEAR LOGIC**

Let me sort out a clear, logical, orderly process. Airs strive for elegance, quality, efficiency and safety. Great at analysis, they are often the first to identify the dangers and how to avoid them.

 Water: **CALM FEELINGS**

Together, we can find the path of least resistance. By considering everyone's feelings and exploring all the available choices, Waters find a way to flow calmly and collectively toward the destination.

 Fire: **BRIGHT POSSIBILITIES**

Let's go! It'll be great! Fires always see the bright side, the possibilities. They are full of new ideas and are confident that if any problems arise, solutions will spontaneously come to light.

What Does the Future Look Like?

When different people look at the same thing from different points of view, then build a composite picture, we can expect a much more realistic result.

Preparation

The group agrees on:

- A time in the future to focus on. (eg. 12 months, 3 years, etc.)
- The breadth to consider – organization/division/team.
- A time frame for the Visioning Process. (eg. 1 hour)

Visioning Process

Having divided into Element groups:

- Imagine a snapshot of the agreed future point in time.
- Answer the *Visioning Questions* (following) for just your own Element of the team vision. For example, Earth answers only the *Firm Outputs* questions.
- Present your view to the rest of the team.
- Discuss as a whole team how the four views can be integrated into a composite shared vision.

The TetraMap® of Vision

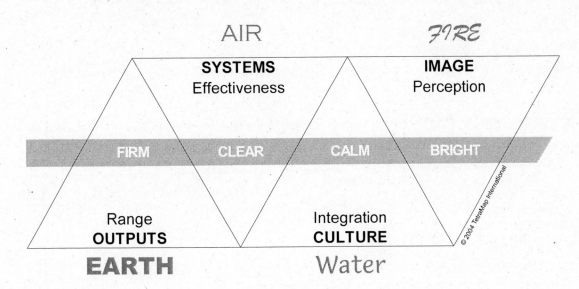

AIR	FIRE
SYSTEMS Effectiveness	**IMAGE** Perception
FIRM — CLEAR	CALM — BRIGHT
Range **OUTPUTS**	Integration **CULTURE**
EARTH	Water

© 2004 TetraMap International

V isionary
I ntent
S hows
I n
O ur
N ature

Multiple perspectives add depth and meaning. A compelling vision for a point in time in the future should consider a:

○ Firm range of intended outputs.

○ Clear effectiveness of the intended systems.

○ Calm integration of the intended culture.

○ Bright perception of the intended image.

Visioning Questions

The different Element groups are typically passionate about their own perspectives. However, they soon realize that the others' perspectives will be vital to the success of their own and when integrated, create a holistic vision for all.

 Earth: **FIRM OUTPUTS**

What will the range of our outputs look like? What products and services will have been cut, modified or created?

 Air: **CLEAR SYSTEMS**

What will the effectiveness of our systems look like? What policies, procedures or technology will have been cut, modified or created?

 Water: **CALM CULTURE**

What will the integration of our culture look like? What behaviors will be demonstrated or eliminated?

 Fire: **BRIGHT IMAGE**

What will our perceived image look like? How do we want our stakeholders to perceive us?

How are we going to Get There?

Having imagined the future result, what process will give us the best chance of achieving it? Combining the Elemental strengths, we can plan a balanced strategy for implementing the vision.

To plan a balanced strategy for implementing the vision:

- One person stays in each group to champion the Element vision, and everyone else mixes into different groups.
- Each group deals with one Element of the team vision and answers all the *Planning Questions* (following) for that perspective.
- At least the first *Action Step* is recorded.
- Each group presents their strategy to the rest of the team for discussion.

The TetraMap® of Planning

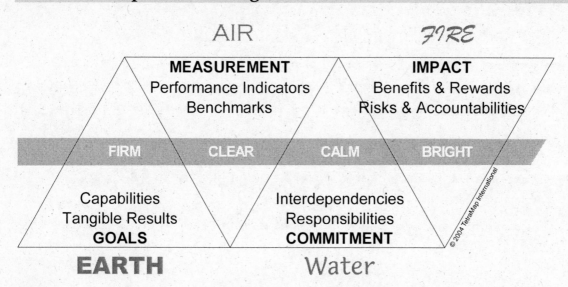

Holistic planning considers all aspects.

P L A N
Planning
Links
Action and
Necessity

○ Firm goals expressed as tangible results within the capabilities of the implementers.

○ Clear measurement expressed as performance indicators for comparison with benchmarks.

○ Calm commitment expressed as responsibilities and their interdependencies.

○ Bright impact expressed in terms of benefits/risks and rewards/accountabilities.

Planning Questions

Focus on:
 Result and process
Quality and quantity
Commitment and recognition
Positive and negative possibilities

 Earth: **FIRM GOALS**

○ What firm goals can we set?

○ How will we know we have achieved each goal?

○ What capabilities and resources do we need to acquire?

 Air: **CLEAR MEASUREMENTS**

○ What clear measurements can we make?

○ What performance indicators can we use to monitor progress?

○ What standard benchmarks do we compare our achievements to?

 Water: **CALM COMMITMENTS**

○ What calm commitments are needed?

○ Who will carry the primary responsibilities?

○ Who are we dependent on and where do we need to build alliances?

 Fire: **BRIGHT IMPACT**

○ What is the bright impact of reaching the goal that will motivate us?

○ What rewards and benefits are possible if we achieve the goal?

○ Who is accountable for managing the risks?

Action Step

To make it real, we must get specific about who, what, when & why. See the following page for an example layout to record actions. An Action Step sheet should be used to record the following:

Action Name A label to identify the action and the strategy it is part of.

Champion Who is going to make sure the action is initiated and followed through?

Who What Where When Specifically, who will do what, where and when?

Evidence What evidence will show the action is a) initiated b) completed?

Carrot Why this action is worth the effort. What's in it for each stakeholder? What will we celebrate?

Note that:

○ The Champion should be present in the room, but need not be directly involved in the action itself.

○ Action Sheets should be copied – one copy is given to the Champion and the other kept for project management.

ACTION NAME

CHAMPION

WHO, WHAT, WHERE, WHEN

EVIDENCE OF INITIATION

EVIDENCE OF COMPLETION

CARROT

Empowering Leaders & Followers

The process ends with people declaring their commitment to the vision:

○ I have the courage and determination to…

○ I have the wisdom and knowledge to…

○ I have the compassion and insight to…

○ I have the vision and inspiration to…

The TetraMap® of Leadership

Leaders

Enable

And

Demonstrate

Elemental

Respect

A strong leader of high integrity leads from both the front and the back and combines the strengths from each Element of the TetraMap.

○ Firm, determined courage.

○ Clear, knowledgeable wisdom.

○ Calm, insightful compassion.

○ Bright, inspiring vision.

The Nature of Leadership

Does your leadership reflect Nature?

 Earth: **FIRM COURAGE**

A courageous leader must have the determination to overcome challenges. A leader is like a mountain:

- ○ **Solid** Strength and power is deeply embedded, not easily eroded.
- ○ **Peaked** Clearly demonstrates the direction to head towards
- ○ **Steadfast** Unswayed by the current climate.
- ○ **Lofty** Looked up to for influence.

 Air: **CLEAR WISDOM**

A wise leader must have the knowledge to create a sound strategy. A leader is like the night sky:

- ○ **Vast** Encompasses everything in a focused direction.
- ○ **Principled** Individual points follow a consistent path.
- ○ **Dark & Light** Includes both black and white, side by side.
- ○ **Patterned** Many bright points related by creative analogy.

 Water: **CALM COMPASSION**

A compassionate leader must have the insight to empower followers. A leader is like a lake:

- ○ **Quenches Thirst** Revives and re-energizes.
- ○ **Mirrors** Provides a different perspective.
- ○ **Collects** Includes input from all directions without bias.
- ○ **Magnifies** Makes larger than life.

Fire: **BRIGHT VISION**

A visionary leader must have the inspiration to create a compelling future. A leader is like a bonfire:

○ **Hot** Raises the energy level.

○ **Mesmerizing** Attracts and focuses attention.

○ **Multisensory** Noticeable to a broad range of senses.

○ **Radiant** Visible from afar, from all directions.

Natural Outcomes

With natural intentions, we can hope to achieve synergistic outcomes. We can also expect natural unpredictability and diversity. Although we may prefer the simple binary symmetries of black and white, good and bad, right and wrong, we know that Nature works in continuous shades.

The TetraMap offers multiple frames of reference to ensure that we grasp more opportunities for success. It is a thinking habit that will help us to approach people and situations with open minds and open hearts.

Our intention for the TetraMap is to provide a new mental model for finding natural, holistic solutions and reducing conflict in all our communities.

As Yodimi, (Yoda's Grandmother) always said:

May the Natural Force be with you.

TetraMap® Resources

Resources based on the TetraMap are available from www.tetramap.com.

Why Are You Like That?

Workbook Materials

AN ADVENTURE INTO THE NATURE OF BEHAVIOR

Workbook, Folding TetraMap & Element Sticker

The 22 page *Workbook* includes • a self-scoring questionnaire, • a description of the TetraMap® of Behavior model, • exercises to build on personal and team strengths. Insightful reading before, during *and* after training sessions. Available in English, French, German, Spanish.

The *Folding TetraMap* is a 5 inch full-colour, die-cut cardboard model that demonstrates the physical properties of the model. Have participants fold their own tetrahedron models and use them as dice or Element indicators. The blank reverse is ideal for note-taking.

Each *Element Sticker* includes four 1 inch square labels ideal for sticking on name tags or directly on clothing.

Also available as:
• *Workbook 100 Pack* (100 sets of Workbook Materials)
• *Workbook & Sticker* (ie without the Folding TetraMap)

Why Are You Like That?

Premium Pack

FACILITATING AN ADVENTURE INTO THE NATURE OF BEHAVIOUR

A comprehensive set of resources, including *Workbook Materials* for 20 participants and the *TetraMap Book.*

An 86 page *Leader Guide* includes a storyboard of the PowerPoint Presentation which can be used to run the *Why Are You Like That?* activity and to explain the TetraMap model. Animation and colourful visuals give impact to the explanation, and stimulate interactivity.

A CD-ROM with the PowerPoint Presentation includes: *Islands of Opportunity* (see below), *Key Know* (see below), *Caricature Posters* for lively signage or decoration.

Starter Pack

VALUE DIVERSITY AND CREATE SYNERGY

Mini Guide plus *Workbook Materials* for 10 participants

The guide describes how to facilitate a fun, highly interactive 50-120 minute activity for improving communication and relationships within a group. Includes further information on the model.

About the Authors

TetraMap International Directors, Yoshimi and Jon Brett have been studying the Four Elements concept for over 20 years, and first published the TetraMap version in 2000. Their Workbooks have enabled thousands of people to understand the value of natural behavioral styles. Yoshimi & Jon continue to offer workshops to support teams while developing further resources based on the TetraMap.

Yoshimi, is a Japanese American New Zealander. After 8 years as a teacher, she joined Jon on a sailing adventure in the South Pacific and finished the trip off in Japan studying the language and music. Yoshimi spent the subsequent 20 years in the business world, focussing on health, recreation, the environment and organizational development. She is a compassionate, right-brain facilitator with a great sense of fun.

Jon has a BSc, and also began in teaching. He then took on a technical writing career, writing user manuals for computer systems until he teamed up full time with Yoshimi in 1995. Jon is a more left-brained desktop publisher and webmaster, with a great sense of how to catalyze learning.

www.tetramap.com

Visit the TetraMap web site for resources and Facilitator programs.